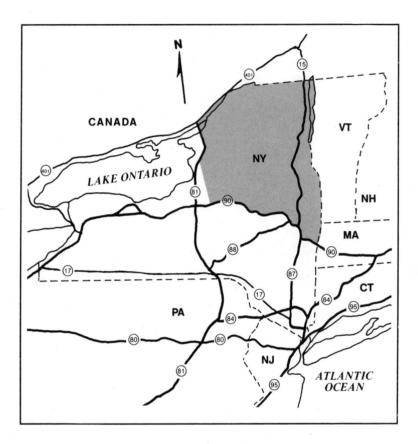

GOOD FISHING
in the Adirondacks

THE GOOD FISHING IN
NEW YORK SERIES

GOOD FISHING

in the Adirondacks

From Lake Champlain to the Streams of Tug Hill

Maps Created by Larry Boutis
Drawn by Jim Capossela

A Jim Capossela Book

Dennis Aprill
Editor

Backcountry Publications
Woodstock, Vermont

Good Fishing in the Adirondacks was first published in 1990 by Northeast Sportsman's Press and Stackpole Books (ISBN-8117-4017). This second printing by Backcountry Publications has been carefully updated.

Library of Congress Cataloging-in-Publication Data

Good Fishing in the Adirondacks : from Lake Champlain to the streams
    of Tug Hill / Dennis Aprill, editor : maps created by Larry Boutis ;
    drawn by Jim Capossela.
        p.   cm. -- (The Good fishing in New York series)
        Originally published: Tarrytown, N.Y. : Northeast Sportsman's
Press, 1990.
        Includes index.
        ISBN 0-88150-236-7 : $15.00
        1. Fishing--New York (State)--Adirondack Mountain Region.
    2. Fishing--New York (State)--Adirondack region-
    -Guidebooks. I. Aprill, Dennis. II. Series.
    SH529.G66 1992
    799.1'1'097475--dc20   92-14667
                                                                              CIP

Published by Backcountry Publications
A division of The Countryman Press, Inc.
Woodstock, Vermont 05091

Printed in the United States of America
10-9-8-7-6-5-4-3-2

Acknowledgements

Because of the large number of authors involved with this book, it is not possible to list all of the dozens of people who helped with its preparation. The publisher would therefore like to offer a blanket thank-you to all those kind individuals, and add a special thanks to the helpful people in the Adirondack offices of the New York State Department of Environmental Conservation.

Credit must also be given to the photographers whose work added greatly to the project. They are: Dennis Aprill (pages 50, 66); Allen Benas (161, 176, 224); Jim Capossela (54, 57, 65, 82, 103, 184, 200); Pete Casamento (20 –both, 117, 146); Jim Gould (87); Joe Hackett (85, 139, 209); Ron Kolodziej (152, 153); New York State Department of Environmental Conservation (22, 76); *Plattsburgh Press Republican* (66); Marty Rosencrantz (30, 38); Alice Vera (72, 80, 127); Robert Zajac (130); and Tony C. Zappia (203).

Warning!

The New York State Department of Health warns that many fish in New York waters contain certain potentially harmful contaminants. You are advised to consult the New York State Department of Environmental Conservation for further details. Many of the current advisories will be seen on the inside of the front cover of the DEC annual publication *New York State Fishing Regulations Guide*.

Contents

Maps

MAP LEGEND

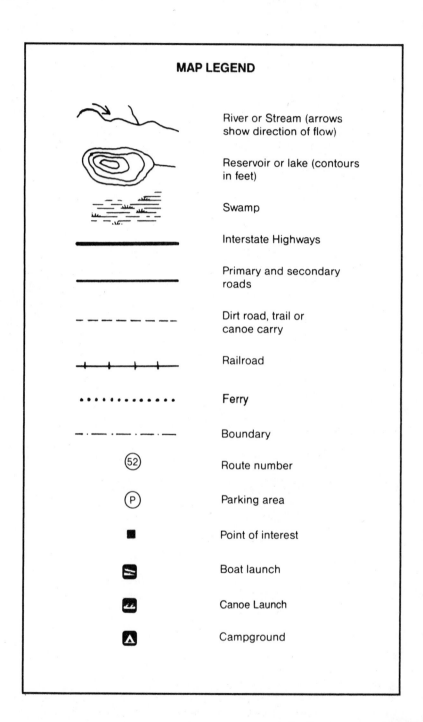

River or Stream (arrows show direction of flow)

Reservoir or lake (contours in feet)

Swamp

Interstate Highways

Primary and secondary roads

Dirt road, trail or canoe carry

Railroad

Ferry

Boundary

Route number

Parking area

Point of interest

Boat launch

Canoe Launch

Campground

Approximate Geographical Locations of the Maps Presented in This Book
(For page numbers turn back to p. xi.)

Notes on map legend, facing page:

No attempt was made to show all boat/canoe launches, or campgrounds. Only very select points of interest are depicted on the maps in this book. Not all secondary roads are shown. Not all trails are shown, and locations of trails may not be precise.

About the Editor

Dennis Aprill, when not teaching English and journalism at SUNY, Plattsburgh, uses his spare time writing outdoor articles and fishing. Since 1980, he has published articles in *Adirondack Life, The Conservationist, Country Journal, Maine Life, New York Alive* and *Sports Afield.* He is also the outdoors columnist for the *Plattsburgh Press Republican* and co-author of *Mammals of the Adirondacks.*

Dennis describes himself as a "subsistence angler" who enjoys working the small mountain streams and beaver ponds in search of native brook trout. He has also fished extensively in northern Ontario, Quebec and Labrador and has presented talks and slide shows to Trout Unlimited and other groups on the fishing opportunities in these regions.

Dennis lives with his family in a remote area in northeastern New York State.

Acid Rain

One of the most immense environmental problems of our age is acid rain, also called acid deposition. The Adirondacks is one of the areas of North America that has been hardest hit by this insidious menace, and the publicity has led many anglers to believe that most Adirondack waters are "dead." This is far from the case, since good fishing still abounds in stream and pond, lake and river. Yet it is true that about 200 high-elevation ponds here have been wiped out by acid rain and that about 300 more are threatened. In addition, certain headwater tributary streams have been affected to the point where fish life has been greatly diminished or even eradicated.

Acid rain stems from the chemical reaction of sulphur and nitrogen oxides with water in the atmosphere. These chemicals are primarily released into the atmosphere via the smokestacks of factories and the tailpipes of motorized vehicles. Basic high school chemistry demonstrates that when you combine the oxides of these chemicals with H_2O you get H_2SO4 and HNO_3, or sulphuric acid and nitric acid. Here in the late twentieth century it is literally raining (and snowing) acid. Not only has this hurt aquatic life, but it is now starting to slowly kill some of our higher elevation forests. It is safe to assume that as acid rain worsens – and the woeful "wait and see" attitude of the federal government has assured that it will – its direct impact on human health will be exacerbated.

The relative acidity or alkalinity of any solution depends upon its concentration of hydrogen ions. It is expressed as a number on a logarithmic scale ranging from 0 to 14. A pH of 7.0 is neutral. A change of one pH unit, for example from 6.0 to 5.0 indicates a tenfold increase in hydrogen ion concentration. Normal rain water is 5.6. The pH of acid rain is lower. How much lower determines the magnitude of the threat. In the mid-1970's, the mean pH of 214 high elevation Adirondack ponds was about 4.75. Some species can tolerate (at least in the short term) this degree of acidity, but most cannot. Anything below 5 is generally bad news.

And that leads us to the classifications used in dealing with acid rain. Waters having a pH of 6.0 or higher are considered "satisfactory." Those between 5.0 and 6.0 are considered "endangered." Those below 5.0 are termed "critical."

In a survey that took place between 1975 and 1982, 1,047 Adirondack lakes and ponds were sampled. This is about 38% of the 2,759 ponded waters located within the region (transitory beaver and bog ponds would push that 2,759 figure higher). All the sampled waters fell within a modified 1,000-foot elevation perimeter which roughly coincides with the Adirondack Park boundary. Approximately 92% of the estimated 246,271 acres of ponded water within the zone were sampled. The results were as follows:

Waters	(%)	Classification	Acres	(%)
199	(19.0)	Critical (below 5.0)	8,796	(3.9)
264	(25.2)	Endangered (5.0-6.0)	23,346	(10.3)
584	(55.8)	Satisfactory (above 6.0)	193,710	(85.8)

More recently (1984-1987 and ongoing) surveys done by the Adirondack Lake Survey Corporation covered 1,469 ponds or lakes. Of these, 1,123 contained fish while 346 were without fish. In looking at these two surveys, though, it should be remembered that undoubtedly some of the now fishless ponds never did contain fish.

In spite of that qualifier, there is no denying that acid rain has either wiped out or reduced the fishing opportunity on somewhere between 15-25% of fishable Adirondack ponds. The surveys have shown that ponds smaller than 50 acres and at elevations greater than 2,000 feet are at greatest risk. Though less studied at this point, certain smaller streams at higher elevations have also been seriously affected. Taking a region-wide look, we see that waters in the southwestern Adirondacks have been hardest hit. This is partially because of higher precipitation levels in this part of the Adirondacks. As an example, many ponds and lakes just north of Stillwater Reservoir, including ones in the scenic Five Ponds Area, have been strongly affected.

Backpacking in for native brook trout is an old Adirondack tradition, and is well covered in this book. Yet it is clear from the preceding discussion that an angler heading out into the brush by foot or by canoe should find out which ponds to avoid. Here, the New York State Dept. of Environmental Conservation can help.

Regional DEC offices in Ray Brook, Warrensburg and Watertown (for location see the appendices) can provide specific information on most waters within their jurisdiction for which current survey data exists. Other information, including scientific reports on acid precipitation can be obtained by writing to the DEC Survey and Inventory at Ray Brook, NY 12977. One type of computer listing available to the public will be an annual update of "critically" acidified waters.

Introduction

Imagine for a moment that you are suspended 30,000 feet directly above Mt. Marcy, New York State's highest mountain. The high peaks appear as a somewhat off-center hub of a gigantic wheel with rivers radiating like spokes towards every point on the compass. Flowing north you would see the Raquette and St. Regis; to the east the Saranac, Ausable and Boquet; to the south the Schroon and the Hudson; and to the west the Moose and the Beaver. From this preferred vantage point not only would you start to get an idea of the immensity and wildness of the region, but a peculiar geological truth might sneak into your consciousness: The Adirondacks are a large dome eroded away (though certainly not uniformly) in every direction by flowing water.

If the day were especially clear, you might even be treated to the sight of two gigantic lakes to the east and south; to a spider web of streams laced across an elevated land mass to the southwest; to a huge river to the northwest. Lake George, lake Champlain, Tug Hill, the St. Lawrence River – all these tempting possibilities might come into view. And then another reality would hit home: There is an awful lot of water just outside the Adirondacks. In all directions, as a matter of fact.

This book, then, is about fishing in northern New York, roughly that area north of the Thruway. It focuses not only on the wild and beautiful central Adirondacks, but also on the vast water systems on the fringes. Through the voices of 16 local writers, all of whom live in northern New York and many of whom were born here, it takes you to remote brook trout ponds and intimate streams. It leads you to larger blue-ribbon fly fishing rivers. It guides you to crystalline lakes where swim lake trout, salmon, bass, muskies, pike and much more.

With a culture and a history both unique and varied, this great wilderness of the east has been consecrated by artists in every possible medium: Photography, painting, poetry, mountain crafts, and, of course, writing. It is still a beautiful, lightly settled region – only 120,000 people live full time within the Adirondack Blue Line – and it's so inspiring that a modern day angler might yet share the sentiments of W.H.H. "Adirondack" Murray, who described in *Adventures In The Wilderness* the first morning of an Adirondack fishing adventure more than a century ago:

> How cool the water; how fresh the air; how clear the sky; how fragrant the breath of balsam and pine; O luxury of luxuries, to have a lake of crystal water for your wash bowl, the morning zephyr for a towel, the whitest sand for soap and the odor of aromatic trees for perfumes! What belle or millionaire can boast of such surroundings?

1

THE GREAT INLAND SEA
part one
by Bernie Jandreau

Grandly situated between the majestic Adirondack Mountains and the Green Mountains of Vermont lies beautiful Lake Champlain. At any mid-lake vantage point, one is treated to an awesome panoramic display of lofty peaks flowing down to lush green valleys bordering on the edge of shimmering blue.

Often called the sixth great lake, Champlain boasts 585 miles of shoreline, 435 square miles of water, and 110 miles of length from its southern terminus at Whitehall, New York to its outlet at the Richelieu River just north of the Canadian border. Its maximum depth of 401 feet can be found at the lake's widest point between Port Kent, New York and Burlington, Vermont — a distance of eleven miles.

Many islands dot the surface of Lake Champlain, some of them huge and some of them very small. A host of them are rookeries for various species of wild birds, especially the Four Brothers Islands just south of Willsboro Point. Seagulls, great blue herons and cormorants are nesting guests here and mid April through May can be a bird watcher's paradise.

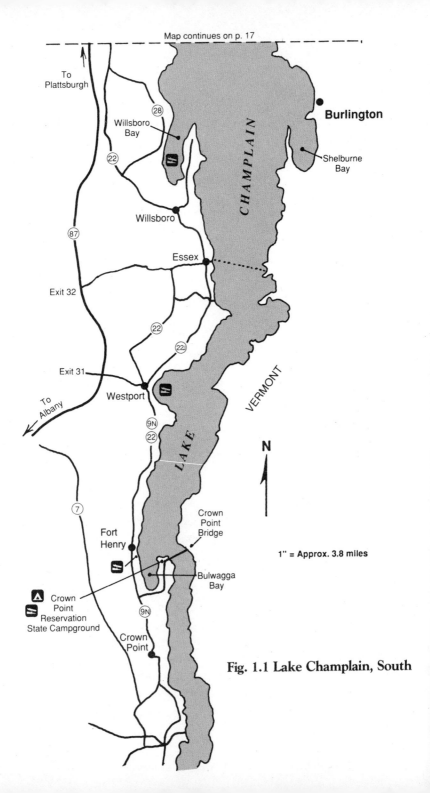

Map continues on p. 17

To Plattsburgh

㉘

Willsboro
Bay

㉒

Burlington

CHAMPLAIN

Shelburne
Bay

㊼

Willsboro

㊿

Essex

Exit 32

㉒

㉒

㉒

Exit 31

VERMONT

To Albany

Westport

⑨N
㉒

N

LAKE

⑦

Crown
Point
Bridge

Fort
Henry

1" = Approx. 3.8 miles

Crown
Point
Reservation
State Campground

Bulwagga
Bay

⑨N

Crown
Point

Fig. 1.1 Lake Champlain, South

As one might guess, the prospect of water sports is as intriguing to many as is the beautiful scenery. Sail and power boats are seldom in short supply on the lake, but with a body of water this size they are usually of little concern to the fisherman. An imaginary line separating the states of New York and Vermont extends the entire length of the lake. As there is no reciprocal agreement between the two regarding fishing rights — although there may be soon — it is wise to buy a Vermont fishing license if you plan to spend any time here. Lacking that, purchase lake charts which show the boundaries. The lake is very narrow at both the north and south ends, and one could easily venture into the other state's water without realizing it.

In this chapter we will be dealing exclusively with the "cool water" species of Lake Champlain, since the cold water species are discussed in Ch. 2. Our discussion will take us up the western shore of Champlain from Ticonderoga, NY, all the way to the Canadian border, a distance of about 100 miles. For your fishing information, I will name several tributaries as well as launch ramps, shore fishing sites and nearby towns and villages for supplies and accommodations. It will be helpful to look back and forth at the maps, Figs. 1.1 and 2.1.

Before we start our trip, a word of caution: If you plan to fish the lake from a boat, be sure to have proper working safety equipment. My 50 years of experience on this lake have taught me many lessons. A peaceful, sleeping beauty can suddenly turn into a raging witch. Carry items like a weather radio, flare kit, life jackets, fire extinguisher, anchor, oars, rain gear and an auxiliary motor if you have one. And by all means, the larger the boat the better. I am not implying that the lake is always treacherous. I'm merely pointing out that it can get rough out there, especially in the summer when sudden storms out of the west are down on you before you've had a chance to take cover. There are more calm, relatively placid days than bad ones, though.

Your fishing opportunities on Lake Champlain are super. With some 23 cool water species, you have the kind of variety that is found in very few other waters in the northeast. In this chapter we will deal mainly with the most popular species: black bass, northern pike, walleyed pike, pickerel, muskellunge and certain of the more popular panfish.

At the village of Ticonderoga, look for the signs directing you to the ferry to Vermont. The state boat landing is adjacent to the ferry landing. The ramp is good, with plenty of parking. The village of "Ti" can take care of all your boating and fishing needs, as well as food and lodging. Historic Fort Ticonderoga overlooks the lake and is a must-see attraction. All this is just minutes away from the ramp.

Some excellent fishing for bass, both largemouth and smallmouth, can be found in the vicinity. As this end of the lake is narrow and shallow, you will find lots of weedbeds and lily pads with the result that the largemouth predominates. Live minnows, spinnerbaits, surface lures and rubber worms will work best for you here.

Northern pike, pickerel, walleyes, perch, crappies and sunfish are also found throughout this area. The same lures mentioned above will take the pike and pickerel, and some panfish. Trolled nightcrawlers or minnows are good for the walleyes, while a can of garden worms is still best for the little fellows.

The best time to fish this area is from mid May through mid-October, although some great ice fishing can be had all winter. As is the general rule, boat fishing is always the best way to cover the most water, even though some limited bank fishing is available.

Moving north we enter the village of Port Henry. An excellent, well maintained state launch ramp is located right in the heart of town. All facilities are at your fingertips and the fishing is very good nearby. Five miles in either direction (north or south) from the launch ramp will provide you with plenty of good fishing for all species mentioned above. In addition, cold water fish such as lake trout, landlocked salmon and a stray steelhead now and then will turn up.

Looking southeast to south from the launch ramp you will see the Crown Point Bridge and Bulwagga Bay, two excellent fishing areas. The bridge abutments hold some fine smallmouths, while in the deeper water under this span you will often find some good trolling for walleyes.

Adjacent to the bridge on the southwest side is the Crown Point Reservation State Park and Campground, a nicely maintained scenic facility overlooking the lake. A T-Shaped covered pier here extends a few hundred feet into the lake and is a good spot to catch some panfish and an occasional bass or pike. A small launch ramp is located about 100 yards from the pier and is available to anyone using the park. A small park entrance fee is charged.

Bulwagga Bay is just ¼ mile west of the bridge and is a haven for largemouth bass, pike and pickerel. Panfishing in this bay is great for perch, crappie, sunfish and bluegill. The bay is easily identified as it adjoins the main highway (Rt. 22 north) into Port Henry and the launch ramp.

As you enter the bay you will see a large section of riprap on the right side. Smallmouths and an occasional largemouth will be holding on these rocks. The entire perimeter of the bay will be grassed over by mid-summer with an open channel down the middle. Pike, pickerel and largemouth will be holding in or near this grass.

On the left side of the bay as you enter you will see a short peninsula of rocks jutting out towards the center of the bay and marked by warning buoys. Don't pass up this area. The south side drops off into 15 to 20 feet of water at the end and the bottom works gradually up to the main shoreline. Weed beds abound just off these rocks and a variety of fish, especially largemouths, are abundant. Rubber worms and spinnerbaits have filled my livewell many times here.

To get the most out of Bulwagga Bay, try to get there in May,

Bob Morrison (seated), and noted Lake Champlain guide and author, Don McKee, try for largemouth on expansive Bulwagga Bay. This bay, plus the nearby Crown Point Bridge, are two Champlain hotspots.

June or July. If your fishing trips involve camping, an excellent campground is on the shore at the entrance to the bay. The lake starts to deepen as we go north of Port Henry, so I would concentrate my efforts on Bulwagga Bay, the Crown Point Bridge and south. Weedy coves and rocky ledges are the rule south of the bridge. Add some crankbaits and jigs to your arsenal of lures for the smallmouths hanging around the rockpiles and points in this section. Spinnerbaits and rubber worms will pull the largemouths and pike out of the weedbeds. Best time to fish this general area? Spring through fall.

We now move on to Westport. I won't dwell long on this section as it will be covered in Ch. 2. However, some good smallmouth fishing can be found along the rocky shoreline that abounds in the area. Steep cliffs jut down to rocky points all the way south to Port Henry and north to Split Rock Point at Whallon Bay. Summer and fall fishing is best and a boat is almost mandatory. The launch is located in the village and services are limited to a few restaurants and marinas. Some accommodations are available.

Approximately four miles north of the village of Keeseville flows one of the lake's major tributaries, the Ausable river. During mid summer, the lower section (Rt. 9 bridge to mouth) is barely fishable due to low water. However, spring fishing — mid April through mid June — is excellent for salmon and smallmouth bass. The Ausable and other key Champlain tributaries are discussed at length in other chapters.

Just south of the city of Plattsburgh is the Valcour Island area. This section is prime water for walleyes, smallmouths, and some real big pike. The state launch ramp is conveniently located off Rt. 9 directly across from the island, and has excellent parking and restroom facilities. Several marinas, motels and restaurants are located within yards of the ramp. The island itself is a haven for boaters, not only because it provides shelter during sudden storms but also because of its scenic beauty and sandy beaches. A "primitive" campground (limited facilities) maintained by the state is on the northwest side and is, of course, only accessible by boat.

Valcour's rocky shoreline makes for some good smallmouth bass fishing, and deep water trolling around the island can produce some really big pike. A surprise bonus may also turn up in the form of a big lake trout or a nice salmon.

Most significant in this area is the good walleyed pike fishing. Approximately three-fourths mile north of Valcour Island is Crab Island. Much smaller than Valcour, it provides the necessary line of sight between the islands to place you over the reefs for the best walleye fishing. As walleyes are predominantly night feeders, this kind of fishing is always best after dark. The fish rise at this time from the bottom to feed on baitfish on or near the surface. Lures trolled with small split shot produce well. In the last few years, planer board trolling has really taken off, and has proven itself to be an effective night fishing tool.

Daytime fishing these same reefs will give you some action, but you will have to go deep. Bait walker sinkers or three-way swivel rigs will get you down to the big ones. Perch school up after spawning and move out into the main lake. The bottom structure around Valcour Island is basically rocky with some sandy or pebbly beaches scattered here and there. Locate the school with your depth finder or simply cast to the shoreline as you move around the island. My favorite bait for schooling perch is the Mister Twister Sassy Shad in shad color mounted on a ⅛ ounce jighead. The inch and a half size seems to work best and six pound test performs well with this set-up. You can either swim the lure or jig it. Of course, small minnows and the old reliable garden worm work well also.

Now let us move on to the Plattsburgh and Saranac River area. Flowing through the city, this river has fine spring fishing for salmon, walleye, and smallmouth. Best time is mid April to early June. The salmon arrive first, followed by the walleyes and bass. Like the Ausable, the water recedes in June and so the fish move out early.

All of the fishing is concentrated at the mouth of the river and several hundred yards upstream. Beyond this the river becomes too shallow to navigate and a dam two miles upstream stops all fish progress. Bank fishing is popular here. The city of Plattsburgh offers all services, of course.

If you are fortunate enough to be in this area during the perch spawning season — usually April through the first or second week of May — you're in for a real treat. Just north of the Saranac River is Cumberland Bay. Starting at the Plattsburgh City Beach and running east some two miles to Cumberland Head Point is some of the best spring perch fishing you will find anywhere in the lake. The bottom is rocky and ideal for spawning perch. Huge schools move in here and the action can be fantastic. The same methods I mentioned earlier will work well, just bring along some good-sized coolers because you're going to pick up lots of "slabs."

The next three fishing areas are most important, and are my favorite on the western shore of Lake Champlain. Each abounds with all the cool water species we've been discussing.

First is the Point Au Roche Area. Approximately four miles north of the city of Plattsburgh on Rt. 9 you will find signs directing you to the Point Au Roche boat ramp. The ramp is well maintained and has ample parking along with portable johns. Limited lodging and other facilities are available.

As you look to the northeast from the ramp, you will see an island appropriately named Isle La Motte (which was named after the French Captain Pierre de St. Paul [sieur de la Motte] who commanded the fort built on the island in 1666). Note that this island sits in Vermont waters.

Our fishing areas in this section will extend some two and one half miles south to Treadwell Bay and six miles north to the Little Chazy River. We will be covering various types of fish-holding structure along the way.

Moving south out of the launch ramp you will notice the rocky shoreline almost immediately. This structure continues all the way down to Long Point at Treadwell Bay. Smallmouth bass relate to this structure, so start fishing the shoreline three hundred yards or so from the ramp. Before you venture too far, turn around and notice two red buoys directly behind you. The northernmost buoy marks a small rockpile and almost always has some small-mouths hanging around. The southern buoy marks LaRoche Reef and is excellent structure for walleyes.

Back on the shoreline, cover all the good looking points on your way down to Long Point. The point itself extends underwater almost three-quarters of a mile due south to a red buoy that is visible from the point. Smallmouths will be on top of this structure and walleyes will be stacked somewhere on the sharp drop-off on the east side of the point all the way out to the buoy.

On the inside of Long Point, you will find Deep Bay, Middle Point, and Short Point. Fish all around these points and bays for smallmouth and northern pike.

Now let's move north from the ramp. About a mile north is North Point, known locally as Dicksons Point. Fish the point around into Monty Bay. The point is smallmouth country and the bay is northern pike, pickerel, and largemouth bass territory. The south side of this bay is all weed beds and marsh grass. Check this area out carefully.

Starting at Wool Point on the north side of Monty Bay, work your way to the Little Chazy River. Cover all the rocky points for smallmouths and the many bays for pike and pickerel. The Little Chazy River is exceptionally good for largemouth bass in early spring. About June 15th the river becomes choked with weeds and is impassable by boat. The weedy section at the mouth of the river is fishable most of the season.

My second favorite area is the Great Chazy River and the King's Bay section of the lake. Here, again, there is only limited lodging and other services.

At the mouth of the river you will find an excellent launching ramp maintained by the state. With room enough for 50 cars and trailers, it provides a good jumping off point not only for Kings Bay but all the good fishing areas both north and south of the river. The Canadian border is only five miles up the lake from this point.

The Great Chazy is a spring hotspot and is one of the few tributaries to harbor big muskies. Winding its way four miles up to the village of Champlain (there is a barrier at this point), the river provides good fishing for walleyes, bass, muskies, pike, pickerel and hordes of panfish. Several bank areas are open to panfishing, and the peak time overall will be mid April through early July. Musky fishing is best in September and October.

The river flows into Lake Champlain at Kings Bay, a large, shallow, weedy bay extending a half mile both north and south. One look at this bay is all you will need to picture the potential for bass and pike. Many species of panfish are also taken, both summer and winter. I know of no special hotspots in this bay; you can find fish over its entire length and breadth.

And now last, but by no means least, is the Rouses Point section of Lake Champlain.

As launching ramps are virtually non-existent in this area, I would recommend using the Chazy River Ramp. Several good fishing spots can be found all the way up to Rouses Point, a distance of about five miles.

After rounding Point Au Fer and moving north from the Chazy you will approach the first large weed bed at Catfish Bay. Pike, pickerel, largemouth bass and several species of panfish frequent this area. Good fishing can be had here from early spring throughout the summer and into fall. There is little or no access for bank fishing.

Just to your north is the Rouses Point Breakwater. A few quick casts at the very end will tell you if anybody's home. This breakwater is a good spot for those of you who don't own a boat, since it extends well out into the lake and always has good panfishing if the big boys aren't around. Accessibility by car is at the village limit south of town on Rt. 9N.

As you leave the breakwater, the village of Rouses Point will be spread out before you. The shoreline consists of weedy bays, rocky points and several underwater, rock-filled cribs. A lake chart would be very helpful here. However, a few days of observing other fishermen working this area will give you a pretty good idea of where the big ones are.

One outstanding feature you will encounter is the old railroad bridge crossing, an out-of-use span that runs over to Vermont. The bridge hasn't been used in four or five decades, ever since a fire destroyed a large section off the Vermont shore. But over 7,000 wooden pilings are driven into the lake bottom here, creating some fantastic fish holding structure. Big largemouths, smallmouths, northern pike and many panfish species congregate here to feed on crayfish and the hordes of baitfish that flock to the protective shelter of the pilings.

Fish can be found in and around these pilings most of the summer, but the best time is always early fall — September to mid October. This is the time that the big "hawgs" start to feed heavily, as they attempt to store up fat for the long winter ahead. Live minnows, crayfish, and frogs are great here, as are rubber worms and jig and pig combos. Other than these more or less weedless lures, your selection will be quite limited due to the hook catching nature of the wooden pilings.

The pilings extend from the New York shore to the Vermont shore with a break in the center for boat passage. That break is the dividing line separating the two states.

Slightly to the north of the old railroad bridge is the automobile bridge, opened in September of 1987. The concrete pilings hold some smallmouths and pike as well as various panfish. Structure from the old torn down bridge is only some fifty to seventy five feet to the north, and this also holds some bass and pike.

The Canadian border is now less than one-fourth mile away. On your left will be the ruins of Old Fort Montgomery. The U.S. border is just behind the fort. Good fishing for largemouth bass, northern pike and pickerel will be found in the bays surrounding the fort. Trolling the center channel from the fort back south under the new bridge and on through the cut at the railroad bridge can produce some nice walleyes. Boat traffic will be a bit heavy here, especially on weekends. Try to schedule your trolling trips for weekdays.

The Rouses Point area has given me many pleasurable hours and some great fish. Although the village is relatively small, a few fine restaurants and good lodging are available.

In Lake Champlain, the sixth largest fresh water lake in America — behind only the Great Lakes — the fishing can be not only exceptional but extremely varied. When you consider the beautiful scenery and the many fascinating historic points on or near the lake, you have a fishing vacation package that can rival any in the country.

Bernie Jandreau is a native New Yorker born near the northern shore of Lake Champlain. Having actively fished Champlain since age 5, he has more than fifty years experience on the lake. He has been a fishing guide for the past 18 years, and for the last eight years, Head Guide for the Adirondack-Champlain Guide Service in Willsboro. Now semi-retired, he spends his leisure time guiding, lecturing and writing. He holds several bass fishing titles and has garnered more than 50 trophies.

2

THE GREAT INLAND SEA
part two

by Peter Casamento

In the preceding chapter, much information was given on the impressive dimensions of Lake Champlain and on its primary cool water species. Well, this extraordinary body of water may be the ultimate two-story fishery. Let's now look at the stellar fishing that can be had here for the cold water species.

Lake Champlain probably has as many or more different types of catchable fresh water fish as any lake in the northeast. Land-locked salmon, lake trout, brown trout, rainbow trout, smelt and whitefish are the main cold water species, and these primarily inhabit the middle two-thirds of the lake. Lake trout and salmon are the most abundant of these gamefish. Hundreds of thousands of lakers and landlocks are stocked each year by New York and Vermont, and in addition, fall salmon runs on some rivers have established some natural reproduction.

Lakers average three to eight pounds and a lot of lunkers over ten pounds are caught. The salmon average two to four pounds while mixed in are quite a few six to eight pounders and an occasional trophy over ten pounds. Both rainbows (steelhead) and browns average about two to four pounds with an occasional fish of six to eight pounds.

The states of New York and Vermont recently began the Sea Lamprey Control Project on Lake Champlain, with the Ausable, Saranac and Boquet River deltas treated with lampricides in both 1990 and 1991. Although thousands of the cold water gamefish already are caught and released each year, with lamprey control in place the average size of these fish should increase.

The most abundant cold water species is the smelt. Though not considered a gamefish, it is one of the most popular food fish among the natives. The main diet of the cold water gamefish is the smelt. There are millions in Lake Champlain, and without them, there would not be much of a cold water fishery. Smelt average four to eight inches, but occasionally grow to over twelve inches.

Whitefish inhabit the deep water areas of the lake. Although they are not stocked, there are a lot of these fish in Lake Champlain. Until recently, whitefish were seldom caught and most fishermen did not know they were even there. Fishing techniques used in other lakes across the country are now being used in Lake Champlain, and the whitefish is becoming a popular gamefish, as well as a popular food fish. Whitefish average two to four pounds and can reach a weight of twenty pounds.

SPRING

Ice-out on Lake Champlain is usually in late March or early April and, just like clockwork, the day the ice goes out the salmon are in! This is the best time of the year for catching landlocked salmon in good numbers. These fish, along with the browns and rainbows, concentrate in the mouths of the rivers, and in or around the bays and points near the mouths of the rivers. This time of year the rivers are high from the melting snows, washing lots of food down to the lake. The river temperatures are also quite a bit

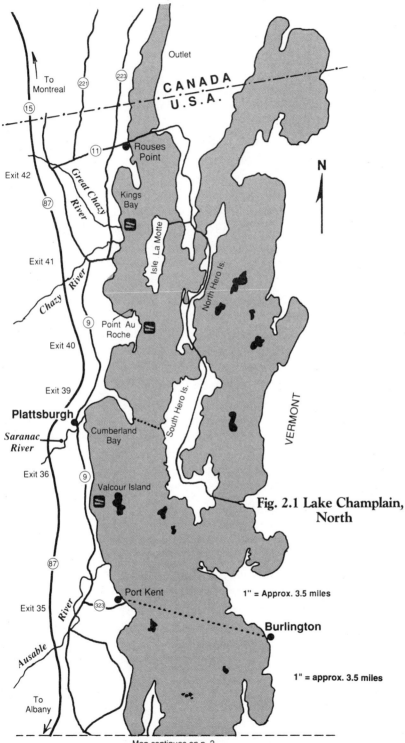

Fig. 2.1 Lake Champlain, North

1" = Approx. 3.5 miles

1" = approx. 3.5 miles

Map continues on p. 2

warmer than the lake temperature; this warmer water really attracts the fish. At this time of year, while the waters are high and murky, fishermen who troll or cast small bright spoons will be the most successful. For the live bait fisherman, worms and nightcrawlers land the most fish.

About late April or early May, when the rains and melting snows have abated, the rivers and streams become crystal clear. This is the time for the lightest line and the smallest lures. Fly casting streamers or trolling streamers with two or four pound test line will catch the most fish. For the bait fisherman, live or dead smelt is best. The best river and stream mouth areas for the salmon and trout at this time of year are the Saranac, Ausable, Boquet, Putts Creek and Lachute Rivers.

From ice-out until mid May, lake trout and whitefish seem to be spread out in deep water. Fishermen using downriggers or lead core line are the most successful. Whitefish are caught on very small spoons and spinners, while the lake trout tend to hit on much larger spoons and Rapala-type lures.

From mid May until late June, the landlocks, rainbows, browns, and whitefish are found near the surface over deep water areas. The Point Au Roche to the Port Henry areas on the New York side are the most productive parts of the lake for these species. Trolling spoons either by flatlining or by the use of planer boards is most productive. Lake trout seem to be at all depths at this time of year and a lot of trout are caught right close to shore in a couple of feet of water near rocky points. Many fishermen cast from shore, or anchor their boats and cast to shore using ¼ to ¾ ounce spoons, while others use dead smelt fished just off the bottom. The most popular points for this shallow water fishing are the Port Douglas to Port Kent area and the Willsboro Point to Westport areas in New York. Fishermen also enjoy success off the many islands and reefs in the lake at this time of year, especially Valcour Island, Schuyler Island, the Four Brothers Islands, Pumpkin Reef, Schuyler Reef, Juniper and Diamond Islands.

SUMMER

About late June, as the surface temperature of the lake rises, the salmon, trout, whitefish and smelt go deep. Downrigger trolling, trolling with lead core line, deep water jigging, or fishing near the bottom with live or dead smelt are the only ways to catch these fish during the summer. Though fish can be graphed over two hundred feet down, most fish are caught forty to one hundred and twenty feet down. Many different sizes and types of flutter spoons, spinners, and minnow imitating lures are used for deep water trolling during the summer. The heavier spoons and bucktail jigs are used for jigging up lakers in deep water. During the hot summer months finding the smelt grounds is the key to catching all the salmonids. Some of the major smelt areas are the deep water areas off the mouths of the Ausable and Boquet rivers, Willsboro Bay/Pumpkin Reef area, Schuyler Reef/Four Brothers Island area, and the Whallon Bay to Westport area.

Next to winter ice fishing, this is the best time of year to catch smelt. Since most of the smelt are concentrated at different depths, jigging with small cut pieces of smelt is the most productive way to fill your bucket.

FALL

Fall is trophy time! Whether you dote on the cool water species or the cold water, fall is the time for catching the biggest of what you're after.

About mid September when the air temperature drops below seventy degrees and the fall rains begin, the rivers and streams bring colder water down to Lake Champlain. The salmon, browns and steelhead sense this and again swim upriver. At this time of year these fish are not going up to feed, but to spawn. Even though the rivers and streams are high, Lake Champlain is about at its lowest level of the year. This means that the lake does not back the mouths of the rivers up as it does in the spring so there is not enough water in the rivers for boat fishing. All of the fishing is done from the banks or by wading using streamers, flies, worms or minnows. Most salmon that go upriver in the fall are four pounds or better.

Since these fish are on a spawning run, they are not feeding. Repeatedly casting or drifting a fly or bait by them is the only way to get them to strike out of instinct or aggravation. All in all, the success ratio at this time of year is lower than in the spring even though the average size of the salmon caught is a lot bigger. Spawning continues through October and into early November. Afterwards, most spent fish make their way back to

Light tackle lake trout is a pleasant reality on Lake Champlain. Casting spoons from shore at the right time and place — especially between Port Kent and Westport — can bring fine action.

the lake where they once again start to feed. The Boquet, Saranac and Ausable Rivers are the very best fall bets for landlocks.

About mid October, the surface temperature of Lake Champlain drops below sixty degrees and once again there is great surface action for lake trout, whitefish and the smaller browns, rainbows, and landlocks. In early November the bigger trout and salmon, which have completed their spawning runs, once again are feeding and are more easily caught. Early November through December is the time to catch the biggest lakers. Mature lake trout, which are six pounds or better, move into the shallow water to spawn at this time. Most spawning takes place in less than ten feet of water. Unlike the other trout and salmon, unless they are actually in the act of spawning lakers will take lures and bait readily. As in the spring, casting ¼ to ¾ ounce spoons will get the big lakers in the shallow water. Trolling flutter spoons, flies, and minnow-type lures will take the most salmon, rainbows, browns, and the smaller lake trout. Fall is probably the best time to get a lot of whitefish, and the right ticket is small spoons, flies, and spinners. Once again, as in the spring most of these fish are caught in shallow water or near the surface over deep water. This action extends right to ice-over, which could be anywhere from late December to mid January.

WINTER

Most parts of Champlain are frozen over by late January. Ice-fishing for smelt, lakers and salmon first starts around the Ticonderoga to Port Henry Area. This area is just south of the deep water smelt grounds where the bottom comes up to about 40 feet. Here the lake is much shallower and freezes over a lot sooner. As soon as the ice is safe enough, the local fishermen are out setting up their shanties. These shanties are mainly set up for smelt fishing. The fishermen jig through holes in the floor of the shanties using hand lines. At the end of the line are one or two single hooks tipped with pieces of cut smelt; above them is a one ounce or more pencil weight. This is the top method for catching smelt on Champlain.

With this method, some lake trout and salmon are taken inci-

When good ice forms on Lake Champlain, "Shanty Town" quickly appears. The delicious smelt is easily the top winter target.

dentally. However, few local ice fishermen try for lakers and salmon. Lake Champlain is virtually untapped for this type of fishing. Tip-up fishing is probably the best way of getting lake trout and salmon in winter and with state regulations allowing 15 tip-ups per person, a fisherman can cover a lot of territory. The best bait to use on the tip-ups is live or dead smelt fished from just under the ice to about 20 feet down. Jigging with special jigging Rapalas, or with other types of ice jigs, is the other way to take these fish.

LURES, BAIT & TACKLE

The basic food fish for the cold water gamefish are the smelt and yellow perch, so any lure or fly that represents these baitfish is a sensible choice. Daredevles, Little Cleos, Krocodiles, Rapalas and Rebels are popular lures; silver, blue and silver, orange and silver, green and silver and gold are the standard lure finishes on Lake Champlain and should be in everyone's tackle box. Another very popular lure is the copper and silver Sutton spoon, which comes in many shapes and sizes. Multi-colored flutter spoons such as the Daredevle Flutter Chucks and the Evil Eye by Red Eye have been very popular and productive in recent years. If you come to Lake Champlain to cast for the lake trout in the spring and fall, make sure you have a lot of red and white Daredevles and blue and silver Little Cleos in the ¼ to ¾ ounce sizes. They are among the most popular and most productive casting lures used on the Lake. Even though I fish for all different species of cold water and cool water fish, in my opinion there is nothing quite like catching them on or near the surface. By using light tackle for surface fishing, you get at least twice the fight out of the fish as you would on heavy tackle in deep water.

Most people who troll for trout and salmon use spoons and minnow imitating lures exclusively, but if you want to increase your success ratio, streamer flies are the answer. Whether you flatline or downrig, there are some days when using trolling flies could mean the difference between getting skunked or limiting out. When trolling in the spring and fall for trout and salmon, I use fly rods or ultralight spinning tackle with four pound leader or line with a number three or number five split shot about eighteen inches up from the fly. Single or tandem flies in most smelt patterns will do. The most popular are the Grey Ghost, Green Ghost, and Nine Three which are smelt patterns. The Mickey Finn and Edson Tiger, Golden Ghost, and Champlain Special are yellow patterns which, I believe, effectively represent the small perch that salmon and trout also feed on.

Nightcrawlers and smelt are the top natural live baits to use in Lake Champlain. Nightcrawlers and ground worms are cast out from the bank or boat and allowed to bounce along the bottom just as would be done in any trout stream. When bottom fishing with smelt, use a whole uncleaned smelt, which will float. Thread an English Gorge hook through the smelt and weight it down with a slip sinker and split shot so that the smelt will float about a foot or two from the bottom. When drift fishing in a boat, use a whole gutted smelt which will sink. Hook it through the mouth and put a sinker about a foot above it.

Use a whole gutted smelt for tip-up fishing, but hook the bait by the dorsal fin so it will hang straight.

LAUNCHING AREAS

There are four major launching sites in the trout and salmon areas of the lake:

1. Point Au Roche Ramp located a few miles north of Plattsburgh (Exits 35 & 36 off the Northway, Rt. 87)
2. Peru Dock which is a few miles south of Plattsburgh (Exits 35 & 36 off the Northway)
3. Willsboro Bay Launch Area (Exit 33 off the Northway)
4. Westport Launch Area (Exit 30 off the Northway)

All these are excellent launching areas with good ramps for almost any size boat and plenty of room for parking.

SHORE FISHING AREAS

Except for the state park areas on Point Au Roche and Ausable Point, most shore fishing areas are owned by the local towns or are privately owned. Moving from north to south these areas are:

1. Point Au Roche Park located a few miles north of Plattsburgh (Northway Exit 40)
2. The mouth of the Saranac River located in downtown Plattsburgh (Northway Exits 36 & 37)
3. Port Kent (Cliff area just south of ferry landing — Northway Exit 34)
4. Willsboro Point, privately owned point with public access (Northway Exit 33)
5. Willsboro/Boquet River below Willsboro Dam (Northway Exit 33)
6. Essex Town Park just south of Ferry Landing (Northway Exit 32)
7. Lachutte River Dam in Ticonderoga (Northway Exits 28 & 29)

The Port Kent and Essex areas are mainly used by the smelt fishermen. No bait fishing is allowed on Willsboro Point. As mentioned above, most of these areas are not state owned so these access areas can be taken away if we don't keep them neat and clean. They are strictly for fishing so no camping or picnicking is allowed.

If you are fishing the Willsboro-Westport area, most accommodations and meals will be found right along Rt. 22. Rt. 9 has a number of restaurants and motels from Keeseville to Plattsburgh. This is the north country's big city and has many motels and restaurants. For a list of accommodations and eating establishments contact these local Chambers of Commerce:

Plattsburgh-Clinton County Chamber of Commerce
Plattsburgh, New York 12901

Willsboro-Essex Chamber of Commerce
Willsboro, New York 12996

Westport Chamber of Commerce
Westport, New York 12993

FISHING SEASONS AND REGULATIONS

Lake Champlain's trout and salmon season is year-round, generally including the tributaries up to the first barrier. The size limit for lake trout and salmon is fifteen inches; for browns and rainbows it's twelve inches. To fish the New York side you'll need a New York license. Once you pass the mid-lake boundary into Vermont you'll need a Vermont license. However at present, New York and Vermont are very close to reaching a reciprocal fishing license agreement for Lake Champlain. The necessary bill has already passed in the NYS legislature, and a corresponding bill is awaiting Vermont legislative approval. In any case, be sure to read the rules and regulations booklet that is issued with your New York State license. There is a specific section in the booklet on Lake Champlain.

Lake Champlain is probably the largest underfished lake in the country, and it offers variety that may not be matched anywhere. I believe the most unique thing about Champlain's trout and salmon fishing is that you can fish for them a good six months of the year right on top, and isn't that the most enjoyable way of getting them?

Peter Casamento is a full-time licensed Adirondack guide and owner of the Adirondack-Champlain Guide Service in Willsboro. Specializing in the Adirondacks and Lake Champlain, he and the numerous other guides who work with him host more than 2,000 sportsmen each year. Peter resides in Willsboro on Long Pond with his wife Jane, daughter Crystal and son Casey.

3

SALMON FEVER!

by Ken Coleman

Of all the great gamefish of North America, few have inspired more admiration, storytelling or sheer awe than the Atlantic salmon, *Salmo salar*. An anadromous fish that lives at sea and spawns annually in fresh water rivers of the northeast, the Atlantic originally moved inland on its spawning runs as far south as the Connecticut River. Over the past 200 years, though, many of the rivers between Maine and Connecticut became unsuitable for salmon due to pollution and dams; the great battler for a long time was pushed northward to New Brunswick, Labrador and Quebec. During the past few decades, however, titanic restoration efforts have re-established small but viable runs in some New England rivers, and the picture has been brightening slowly year by year.

Sometime during the last series of ice ages, *Salmo salar* was cut off from the sea by geological changes, and an inland sub species developed: *Salmo salar sebago*. Happily, many of the same qualities that evoke such passion in Atlantic salmon fishermen are also exhibited by the landlock — streamlined good looks, good fighting ability, a penchant for acrobatics, and a distinguished taste. The largest inland population of landlocks developed in the Great Lakes, where the fish was later eliminated or nearly so by human destruction of that watershed in the 1800's and early 1900's. Similarly, the landlocks which occurred naturally in other large bodies of water in the northeast — for example Lake Champlain — were extirpated by human activity by the mid to late 1800's. Now, landlocks have been reintroduced to several waters in the Adirondacks, and in some of these, limited natural reproduction supported by stocking now occurs. Both Lake Champlain and Lake George offer landlocks, as do several other waters named later in this chapter.

The major concentration of landlocked salmon in northern New York is in Lake Champlain and its major New York tributaries.

First and most important is the Boquet. The Boquet flows from its source in the Adirondack Mountains better than forty miles before it empties into Lake Champlain near Willsboro. Salmon can, with the help of the Willsboro Fish Ladder, ascend as far as the falls in Wadhams, about 12 miles from the lake. Willsboro is in Essex County, about 30 miles south of Plattsburgh and is considered by many to be the center of Lake Champlain's cold water fishery.

The run starts in late April and runs through May with the best fishing in mid May. Water temperature plays a big part in determining when the run starts and ends. The fall run starts in mid September and this is by far the best time to take a big salmon. Each year fish are taken in the seven to nine pound category. With lamprey control now in place, 12 to 15 pound salmon should be possible in the near future. In fact, just a few years ago, before the lampreys became such a problem, some 11 to 13 pound salmon were taken in the Boquet River; the Willsboro Falls Pool was and remains the favorite place of most anglers trying for one of these big landlocks. The fish ladder was not built until the lampreys had taken their toll and the average size started dropping. Now, the ladder may finally make the big impact originally expected of it.

Of the Champlain tributaries, the Boquet offers the most mileage

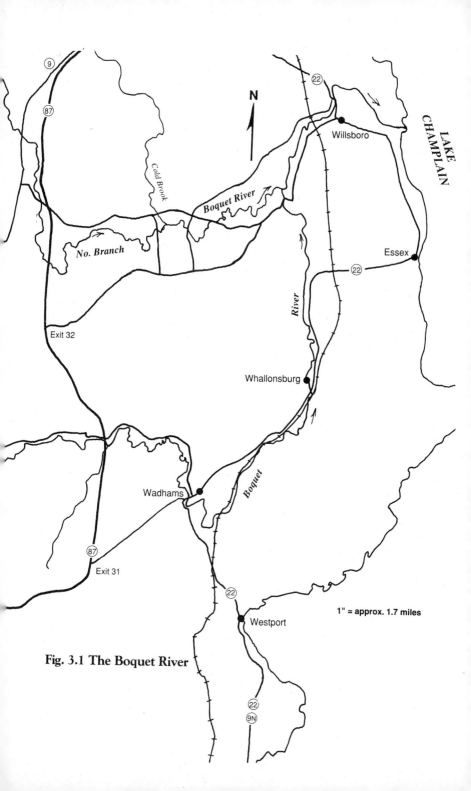

Fig. 3.1 The Boquet River

for fishing and has the most land open to public fishing. Upstream, the falls in Wadhams is a good spot to fish either flies or bait. There is parking along the road or in a lot just south of the bridge on Route 22. Start at the Falls and work your way downstream. There are anglers' parking lots at most of the river crossings, and major pools with enticing water are numerous. Look for holding lies as you work along the stream.

The first fish ladder on the Boquet. Landlocks from Lake Champlain can now ascend the Boquet many miles, making this the top tributary for this exciting gamefish.

Polaroid glasses will help. If you spot a good fish, get above him and work the area with a fly. A good choice would be a Grey Ghost, Black Ghost, or Muddler Minnow.

The North Branch (Fig. 3.1) splits off and offers several additional miles to the angler who enjoys wading and hunting for fish. These upper reaches of the Boquet do not get nearly the pressure the lower part of the river gets, but in turn, contain fewer fish than the lower part. The action picks up fast once you reach Willsboro. There is no fishing from the Rt. 22 bridge to the bottom of Willsboro Falls. This zone protects the fish as they go through the ladder, but the big pool at the foot of Willsboro Falls offers a great place to both fish and ogle at jumping fish as they move upstream. There is a parking lot on the south side of the river. To fish the lower Boquet, head south on Route 22, cross the bridge and turn left; then go by the school and the fish ladder to the lot. From here you can fish the main pool as well as several hundred feet of river below, and in the spring, this is as far as most fish come. Flies and bait are both used here, but day in and day out, more fish are taken on worms and marshmallows than anything else. If you do use a flyrod, this is a great place to fight a big fish.

There are several pools just downriver that offer good fly fishing. Work the pools and riffs slowly with a Grey Ghost, Muddler or your favorite salmon fly. An 8-foot or 8-foot-6-inch fly rod with number seven or eight line is about right. As you move downriver, the water gets deeper and wider and a boat is needed.

To launch your boat, drive by the parking area to the end of the road. There is a parking area and a place to launch a small boat or canoe. From here you can fish to the river mouth and into the lake. If you have a larger boat, you can put in at the State Launch in Willsboro Bay on Lake Champlain and travel down the lake to the river mouth. You could also launch at the Essex Marina and go uplake to the river mouth.

A word of caution for those not familiar with Lake Champlain. On the "Big Lake" — and it is big, over a hundred miles long and eleven miles wide near Willsboro — either a south or north wind can blow up four or five foot waves in a hurry. Don't take it lightly. Boats of 16 feet or less should only be used near shore, and all boaters should keep an eye on the weather. If you can't make it back to the launch, pull into a sheltered bay and wait it out.

Small boats work fine in the river, but should be launched in the river. On a calm day, you can fish the Boquet and out into the lake as far as the marked buoy, and when the wind picks up, move back into the river. These delta areas at the river mouth are shallow and can be fished better by small boats. Bigger boats must be careful not to get hung up on the sandbars.

Watch for fish working on the surface, either cruising or jumping. Use light line and long rods and cast or troll up and down the river. Small spoons and flies or worms take the most fish here. Early morning or late evenings are best, but fish can be taken all day long, and each rain or high water will bring more fish upstream.

One thing about fishing the mouth of the Boquet is that you never know what will hit next. I have taken several nice lake trout while trolling the mouth of the Boquet for salmon, and as the salmon run comes to an end, smallmouth and walleye will move into the river and even a few northerns will be taken at the mouth of the river. Once other fish start moving into the river, the days of the salmon run are numbered.

There are two other major salmon streams along the New York side of Lake Champlain. Like the Boquet, they too have their beginnings in the Adirondacks and flow into Lake Champlain. The Ausable reaches the lake at Ausable Point in Clinton County. Salmon can only run a few miles upstream before coming to the impassable falls at Ausable Chasm, a popular tourist attraction on the edge of the village of Keeseville. The falls here are too high and will forever keep the upper reaches of the Ausable unavailable to salmon. Beyond the abilities of a fish ladder, the falls keep the Ausable limited as a salmon spawning stream.

On the Ausable, most of the land is now private, so wading space is hard to come by. Lots of nice fish, both salmon and trout, are taken off the Route 9 bridge. Spring and fall will find anglers fishing from the bridge. In fact, it is one of the first places I check to see if the fish are running. Worms are the most often used bait here. Flies will work in the big holes near the bridge and some fish-

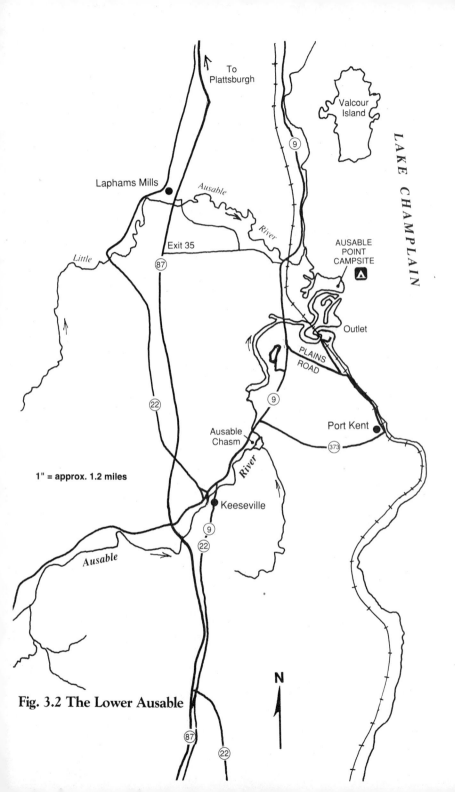

Fig. 3.2 The Lower Ausable

ermen will bring their small boats all the way up here to fish just above, or just below, the bridge. At times they find fast action.

There is a small launch on Ausable Point Campsite Road, and small boats can be launched here or at the end of the point. Larger boats are launched at the Peru Dock, a large State Boat Launch site just above the river on Rt. 9, across from Valcour Island. Lots of fishing takes place around the mouth of both the Ausable, and the Little Ausable which enters Champlain just to the north.

The third great tributary to Champlain, the Saranac, winds its way from the Adirondacks through a series of small dams on its way to the lake. It offers a unique downtown fishery in Plattsburgh, and many nice trout and salmon are taken each year just across from City Hall. There are plans for two fish ladders at the edge of the city, and these would add many more miles of good fishing and spawning grounds for salmon. But for now, the action is confined to the city of Plattsburgh and the lower reaches of the river as the dams form an impassable barrier. The city has had plans for a walkway that would give good access all along the river within the city, but these plans are on hold at this time as budget cuts and pressure from special interest groups have taken their toll. If that walkway is eventually built, it will mean better access and more parking. In fact, original plans called for fish cleaning stations as well. Development like this will be needed if the lampreys are brought under control, because a lot more fishermen will be attracted to the lake and the rivers that empty into it. The other thing the city of Plattsburgh needs is a boat launch that can handle larger boats. There is room for one just north of the river mouth at the old barge dock. This is badly needed because currently, the nearest launch for large boats is several miles away at either Point Au Roche to the north, or south of the city at the Peru dock site. Until it happens, the best spots to fish start at the old dam, which is always a good place to try and a favorite of many fly fishermen.

There are lots of other holes, with the next big favorite being

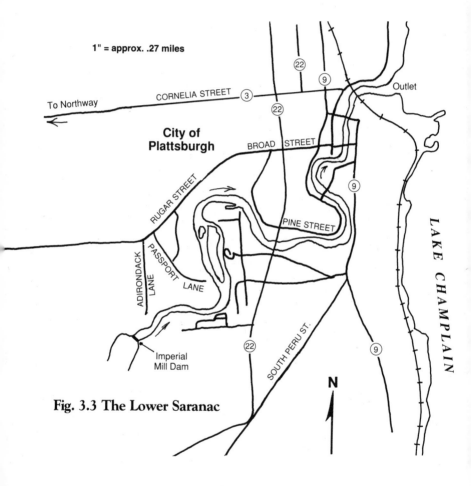

Fig. 3.3 The Lower Saranac

along Pine Street, across from the grocery store and just up from the police station. There is a very large pool here and lots of salmon are taken each year. As you move down, there is another good pool just upstream from Broad Street, behind the Tijuana Jail Restaurant. Next you come to the foot bridge just below the monument. When the fish are in, there will be plenty of fishermen working the pool from this bridge and it makes a good place to check the action and see how the run is going. Just below the bridge is the only boat launch in the city. It will accommodate small to medium boats and offers parking for a limited number of cars. The launch is located on the south side of the river and offers the best access for fishing from here to the river mouth. There is no room to launch big boats — the ramp only accommodates car-toppers or boats 16 feet or smaller. It's a quick, safe way to fish the lower river and believe me, when things are right, it pays off. If the fish are running, there will be several boats both anchored and trolling. Other anglers will be wading, fishing from shore and hanging off the foot bridge. Nothing gets north country anglers more excited than the sight of a leaping salmon, and here is one place where you can see such action in the middle of town.

The lower reaches of all three rivers we've just discussed can be fished by boat. As you work upstream, however, you encounter white water and wading or bank fishing is indicated. There are good runs in both spring and fall and the rivers can be easily fished without a guide. But for those who prefer to use a guide, they are available and can be of great help, particularly on your first trip. Inquire at any area bait & tackle shop.

Whatever your favorite fishing method, you can enjoy these great rivers. Trolling with a fly or spoon is popular off the river mouth, or in the lower river. As you move upstream, many anglers switch to bait such as worms and marshmallows. Fly fishing is very popular in the faster water near the upper reaches of each river.

One note of caution: the Department of Environmental Conservation has placed very restrictive regulations on these rivers from June 15 through December 31 (see the current *New York*

State Fishing Regulations Guide). During this time period it is not legal to use supplemental weights such as split shot, swivels or wire leaders. Only unweighted baits or flies may be used from the lake to the first impassable barrier. The one exception is the Saranac, where floating lures with one free-swinging hook may be used and the no-weight regulations begin at the Catherine Street bridge, rather than at the river mouth.

For a few weeks each spring and fall, the rivers offer the best action, but don't overlook the salmon fishing in Lake Champlain. Chapter 2 discusses that and I'll add only a few personal observations here.

Out on the open lake the fish have lots of room to run, jump, and generally keep your adrenalin flowing. Once in a while, you get one of those special days when the lake is calm and the salmon are right on top feeding on smelt, and this is your chance to fly cast over big water. Use a good smelt pattern and make every cast count. With some luck, you can enjoy the ultimate — a fly rod salmon with lots of room to run and jump. The speed of landlocked salmon is amazing, and don't be surprised if you lose more than you land; its all part of the fun.

I think that one of the most important things to remember whenever you are fishing landlocked salmon is to keep your line light, four or six pound test, and keep your flies or spoons small. A number 12 Grey Ghost with one small weight on a four- pound line can be a real killer. I believe oversized flies or lures with heavy line spook more salmon than anything else. Also important on the big lake is planer boards to keep the line and lure off to the side. That's because as your boat passes over salmon in shallow water, or near the surface, they move to the side. The planer boards take the line to the side and give you a real shot at these fish. This method also lets you run a fly or lure through water too shallow to run your boat in.

Lake Champlain is not the only Adirondack water with landlocks. Lake George, for example, is known to produce some really big fish. So is Schroon Lake and the Schroon River. Then,

A mixed catch of landlocks and steelhead from the Boquet.

there is Upper Saranac Lake in Franklin County, Upper Chateau-gay Lake in Clinton County, and Indian Lake in Hamilton County. All offer good landlocked salmon fishing.

For more information on Adirondack salmon fishing, contact the Department of Environmental Conservation in Ray Brook for the latest list of waters stocked with, and open to, landlocked salmon fishing. New water is stocked from time to time and the DEC lists will keep you up to date. Some of the smaller salmon lakes, by the way, offer great fishing just after ice-out and provide an accommodating setting for the angler with a small boat.

Ken Coleman is a Michigan native who has called New York State home for the last twenty-six years. Currently a Plattsburgh resident, he owns Ken Coleman & Co., a real estate appraisal firm. In addition to writing about hunting and fishing, he has worked to promote the great outdoors through boat shows and through his work with guides and other outdoor professionals in the Adirondack region.

4

THE MIGHTY SARANAC

by John Spissinger

Forget about what you think you're going to catch when you cast into the waters of New York's mighty Saranac River. Ply a small streamer for browns and rainbows in the deep turbulent pockets of the South Branch and your fly might be ravaged by a hungry, deep bodied smallmouth or by an angry northern pike. Troll slowly, or perhaps cast a jig for walleye in Union Falls Pond, and you might have to brace yourself for the dogged, powerful runs of a heavy, lake-reared brown trout. Lob a nightwalker into the smooth currents at the mouth of the river in the city of Plattsburgh, and you just might be treated to the dazzling acrobatics of a fresh-run steelhead or landlocked salmon. Clearly, the rule of thumb to follow when fishing the mighty Saranac is "expect the unexpected."

The Saranac may be unique among Adirondack rivers in terms of the varied opportunities it presents to angling enthusiasts. Not only does it hold an interesting blend of cool and cold water gamefish, it also affords very different types of water that can be fished in different ways according to the individual preferences and skills of the angler. There is plenty of good water to suit the desires of spin, fly, and bait fishermen alike. Public access is excellent throughout the 65 mile stretch of river from Saranac Lake to Plattsburgh. Much of the river is navigable and can be fished from a canoe or small boat. Additionally, there is ample access for wading or bank fishing. Although there are a few seasonal hotspots where anglers tend to congregate, there's enough quality water spread throughout the river to ensure the peace and solitude that many anglers cherish. Combine these features and you have a river that has something to offer every angler.

Located in the northeastern sector of New York's Adirondack Mountains, the Saranac flows easterly through parts of Franklin, Essex, and Clinton counties. Less heralded than its neighbor, the Ausable, the geography of the Saranac has much in common with that other great trout river. The headwaters of the Saranac and Ausable lie but a few miles apart in the High Peaks region of the Adirondack Park. The main stems of both rivers are formed by the confluence of their two branches: the East and West Branches of the Ausable, and the North and South Branches of the Saranac. With Lake Champlain their eventual destination, the rivers traverse roughly parallel courses before entering the lake less than ten miles apart.

Unlike the Ausable, hydroelectric development has had a decisive impact on the Saranac's fishing. More than any other factor, the several hydroelectric impoundments along the Saranac account for the variety, abundance, and local intermingling of cold, cool, and warmwater species of fish. Anglers and environmentalists throughout the country have been rightfully concerned about the detrimental effects of such projects. Frequently, habitat is severely altered or destroyed, and some species of fish are totally eradicated. Occasionally, though, hydro projects have actually had a positive impact upon fishery resources by creating or improving habitat. Arguably, the Saranac is one of those watersheds to have benefitted from its hydro impoundments. Supporting this contention are the fine walleye and smallmouth populations that have developed behind some of its dams, and the establishment of very good brown trout fisheries in the tailwaters below the

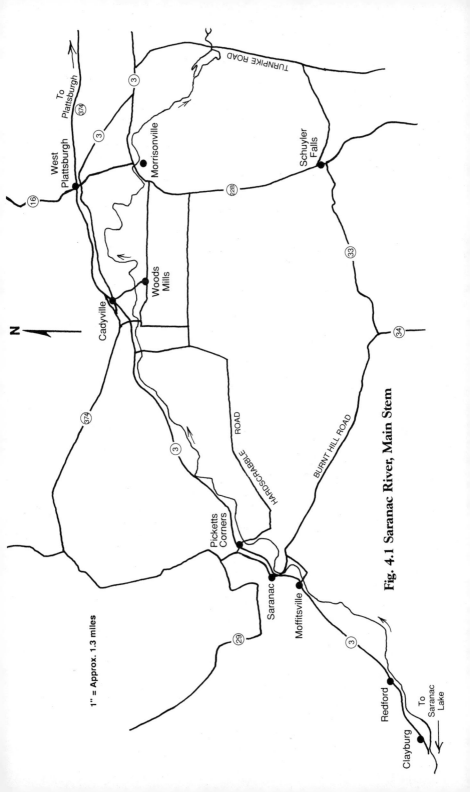

Fig. 4.1 Saranac River, Main Stem

dams, particularly below the Kent Falls dam. Presently, there are nine hydro projects on the Saranac. From a recreational standpoint, the best fishing opportunities are found at Franklin and Union Falls Ponds on the South Branch, and in the waters above the Kent Falls, Mill C, and Cadyville dams on the main stem. Some of the most varied fishing on the Saranac system takes place in the waters above these dams.

Franklin and Union Falls Ponds are both rather sizable bodies of water. Franklin Falls Pond spreads out over 435 acres and has a maximum depth of 30 feet. Larger still, Union Falls Pond encompasses 1,575 acres but is slightly shallower at 20 feet. Both ponds are classified as warmwater fisheries by DEC. (More and more people are using the more accurate phrase, cool water species, and that is the one we use in this book.) An excellent walleye fishery exists in Union Falls Pond, which is stocked heavily with this species. The walleyes are not large, but they are plentiful. Occasional fish are taken in the six to eight pound range. Franklin Falls Pond also supports a walleye population, but it has yet to reach its full potential. However, DEC remains quite optimistic about the prospects for walleye in Franklin Falls, in part because its habitat for this species is actually better than Union Falls.

In addition to walleye, northern pike are prevalent in both ponds. Again, while the fish are not huge, they are abundant and provide excellent sport. Fish in the ten to twelve pound range have been taken, and there are probably some larger specimens lurking in the depths. Smallmouth are also present in good numbers, and there are enough three to five pounders around to keep things interesting. You would not want to fish either Franklin or Union Falls Ponds if brown trout were your primary quarry. Each year, however, both ponds surrender some very large browns that take up residence in the still waters. Besides the gamefish, yellow perch, bullhead, and other panfish provide both action and excellent tablefare. A few of the perch grow to a foot or more, and during the winter they, along with the walleye and northerns, attract a popular following of ice fishermen.

Getting to Franklin or Union Falls Ponds is relatively easy. The River Road in Bloomingdale, the Cold Brook Road in Vermontville, and the Alder Brook Road at the junction of County Route 26, all lead into the area from the south side of Route 3. Yet another route to take, especially if you've been fishing the Ausable, is to drive north on the Silver Lake Road in Ausable Forks to the Union Falls Road near Silver Lake. While private camps dot the shorelines of both ponds, there are plenty of places to fish once there. At Franklin Falls, there are several roadside pull-offs and paths that lead down to the shoreline. Although there are no trailer launch sites, it is quite easy to get into the pond with a canoe or small car-top boat, especially near the dam. Similar access is available on Union Falls Pond. In addition, there is a private launch site and boat livery near the end of the impoundment. If you fish Franklin Falls, don't neglect the deep, slow-water stretch below the dam. Sometimes the walleye, northern and smallmouth fishing here is as good as on the main lake. However, caution should be used when fishing along the steep ledges and rocks above the gorge. Similarly, it is also prudent to be cautious when boating in Union and Franklin Falls as there are boulders and stumps throughout these impoundments. It's a good idea to speak with fellow anglers, or to seek the advice of the proprietor of the launch on Union Falls, to learn where the channels and hazards lie, as well as where the seasonal hotspots are.

The fishing opportunities above the three dams on the lower Saranac, near Cadyville, are similar to those described at Franklin and Union Falls Ponds. Here, though, smallmouth attract the most attention while northerns and walleye play a somewhat lesser role. The reservoirs above the Kent Falls and Mill C dams are quite narrow, at most a few hundred yards wide, and short, about one-half mile long. Behind the Cadyville dam the river is backed up for several miles, although it remains narrow.

Since the Cadyville, Mill C, and Kent Falls dams are not more than two miles apart, it's easy to sample the fishing at each spot on a single day. Route 3 passes alongside the Cadyville reservoir, and intersections with the Harvey Bridge and Goddeau Roads provide access to the Mill C and Kent Falls reservoirs. The New York State Electric and Gas Company (NYSEG) maintains parking areas on both waters. It is possible to put in a canoe or small car-top boat at these sites, though most of the fishing is done from the shore. The village of Cadyville maintains a small recreational area, including a trailer launch facility, right off Route 3. While parking is limited by the size of this facility, it remains a popular access site. Between Cadyville and Saranac, about seven miles upstream, there are several intersecting roads which provide additional access. Some local anglers like to float this stretch, launching their canoes at the Hardscrabble Road bridge in Saranac, and drifting downstream to the Cadyville beach where a second car is left.

The Saranac's reputation as a blue-ribbon trout river is borne out in the productive pools, riffles, and pocket water above and below the several impoundments. Trout fishing enthusiasts can easily explore and sample these stretches by taking a leisurely drive along Route 3, starting either in Plattsburgh or in Saranac Lake. About one-third of the South Branch, half of the North Branch, and virtually all of the main stem border this highway. There are many parking areas along the river which allow you to make close-up inspections of promising stretches of water. Moreover, additional information can be gleaned from local sources like the bait and tackle shops, small grocery stores, inns and campgrounds that are evident along Route 3. Assuming that you're leaving from Saranac Lake, the following paragraphs should give a picture of what to look for as you head downstream.

From the Lake Flower dam to the hamlet of Bloomingdale the South Branch wanders through meadows and swampland. Road access is relatively limited along this slow, deep run, and floating it by canoe is probably the best approach. Although a few trout are stocked in the village of Saranac Lake on a put and take basis, smallmouth and northerns are more numerous. Just before Bloomingdale, the river veers away from Route 3 and quickens its tempo as it flows through pine and hardwood forests. Good access is found along the River Road in Bloomingdale which follows the

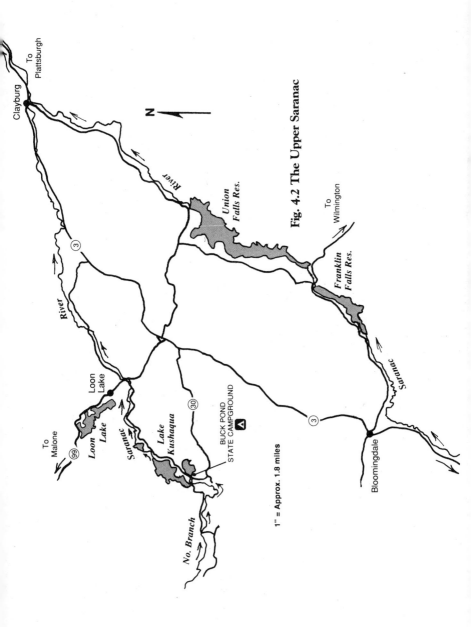

To Plattsburgh

Clayburg

N

River

Union
Falls Res.

Fig. 4.2 The Upper Saranac

To
Wilmington

Franklin
Falls Res.

Saranac

(3)

River

(3)

Loon
Lake

Loon Lake

To
Malone

(99)

Saranac

(30)

Lake
Kushaqua

BUCK POND
STATE CAMPGROUND

1" = Approx. 1.8 miles

Bloomingdale

No. Branch

river downstream to Franklin Falls Pond. Generally, the faster slicks and pocket water hold brown and rainbow trout while a mixed bag is to be found in the slower pools and runs. After passing through Franklin and Union Falls Ponds, the South Branch resumes its course and is largely inaccessible until it crosses the Silver Lake Road bridge. The river is heavily posted and patrolled on both sides of the bridge, but there are three public fishing/parking areas just north of the bridge down to the junction with Route 3 in Clayburg. Anglers must descend steep banks to get to the river from these sites, but the excellent brown and rainbow fishing is worth the effort. This is a turbulent, boulder-strewn section with many deep pockets. Calmer waters are not to be found until the river merges with the North Branch in Clayburg.

For the beauty, solitude and enchantment that so many anglers feel to be the essence of trout fishing, few Adirondack rivers can match the charms of the Saranac's North Branch. It is a cold, quiet little river from its headwaters to its junction with the brawling South Branch in Clayburg. Dense, overhanging alders and waist-deep oxbow bends and undercut banks provide ideal cover for the brook, brown and rainbow trout which thrive in its waters. The river is easy to get to from several well-maintained public parking areas on Route 3, from Clayburg five miles upstream to Alder Brook. During May and June this stretch sees some moderate to heavy angling pressure. Yet few anglers bother to fish the headwaters of the North Branch, which can be reached via the Goldsmith Road which joins Route 3 a few miles west of Alder Brook. The river is much smaller here, in places no more than a few feet wide, and thickly forested. Native brookies are small but plentiful, and occasional wild browns are an added bonus. Although there are a number of private camps and posted property along the Goldsmith Road, DEC has secured public fishing rights in various spots. The fish are highly selective on the North Branch and often you have to work hard to catch them. Still, there are few places anywhere in the region that look as intriguing as the North Branch of the Saranac.

Reasonably good trout water continues on the main stem of the river from Clayburg to Saranac, six miles downstream. Because the river is so broad and shallow here, it doesn't appear to be a productive reach of water. However, the choppy riffles disguise deeper subsurface trenches and pockets. Trout hold in these protected areas and migrate to feed along the shallower edges. Although it takes practice to learn how to read this water, some surprisingly good fishing can be had. Several riverside parking areas are present along this stretch. Generally, the Hardscrabble Road bridge in Saranac marks the dividing line between cold and cool water species. Shortly below the bridge the effects of the Cadyville dam are evident and smallmouth, northerns, walleye and panfish displace the trout.

The final stretch of trout water worth mentioning on the Saranac lies between the Kent Falls dam and the village of Morrisonville. Here the river is broad and fast-flowing, with subsurface runs and pockets interspersed among a few deep pools. Caution should be exercised when fishing this stretch because the water level fluctuates significantly during periods of power generation. The swift currents and loose cobble bottom combine to make wading tricky under any circumstances. The Kent Falls Road borders the river from Route 22B in Morrisonville upstream to the dam. NYSEG maintains a fisherman's parking area below the powerhouse, and some roadside pulloffs give access farther downstream.

Because it is such a large and varied river, the best time of year to fish the Saranac pretty much depends on what you hope to catch and where you plan to go. June and September are probably the best months for both cool and cold water species. Although trout season remains open on a year-round basis, the action is usually better on the lower sections of the main stem in late April and early May, and then improves upstream as the waters warm. During the hottest days of summer the North Branch, with its shaded waters and many spring seepages, is a good bet. Walleyed and northern pike fishing above the dams is best right after the season opens in mid May through June, and then again in the fall. Not to be forgotten is the occasionally excellent ice fishing on

A view of the often tumbling Saranac River, below the rapids at Redford. The young angler will be tested by this heavy water.

Union Falls Pond in February. Smallmouth fishing remains consistently good from opening day in June through October.

If the fish are in a cooperative mood, the flies, lures, and baits that work well for the different species elsewhere are also usually productive on the Saranac. Worms provide the most action since there's not a fish in the river that won't gobble one up from time to time. Live or salted minnows will reduce the number of strikes by nuisance fish like river chubs and improve chances for a good sized northern, walleye, smallmouth or brown. Small jigs, spinnerbaits, plugs and crankbaits also work well for these species. Fly fishermen will encounter many of the major eastern mayfly hatches starting with the hendricksons in early to mid May. The green drake hatch, which begins in early June on the lower river and moves upstream in successive weeks, can be phenomenal. Actually, some of the best smallmouth fishing occurs when this fly is on the water above the dams. Trout will often ignore these juicy morsels and instead feed heavily on smaller caddisflies. But smallmouth find the drakes irresistible and will smash them with a vengeance. Large stonefly nymphs are productive in the South

Branch's pocket water, while terrestrial imitations and midges pay off on the North Branch in summer. As searching patterns, the traditional Adams, Muddler, Hare's Ear nymphs, Ausable Wulffs, and some elk-hair caddis tied in various colors and sizes, will be useful in most situations. With fly patterns as with lures and baits, it's always prudent to compare notes with fellow anglers to learn what seems to be the hot pick at any given time.

Although the city of Plattsburgh marks the end of the Saranac's journey toward Lake Champlain, it is also the site of the newest, and to many the most exciting dimension of the river's diverse menu. In the 1960's New York's DEC began experimental stockings of landlocked salmon in Lake Champlain's major tributaries. Historical records indicate that salmon were once native to the lake, but pollution, overharvesting, and destruction of spawning habitat led to their demise by the mid-nineteenth century. Results of the initial restorative stockings were encouraging as the salmon thrived on the abundant forage base in the lake and then returned to spawn in the lower reaches of the tributaries. The stockings continued throughout the 1970's and 1980's, and were augmented by the introduction of steelhead trout. Today, the Saranac supports moderately good runs of salmon and steelhead. With lamprey eel controls now being used, the prospects for the future will be even brighter, especially if fish ladders are constructed at two hydro dams in and near the city of Plattsburgh.

Salmon and steelhead fishing on the lower Saranac is very different from that found on Lake Ontario's tributaries. Unlike the monstrous chinook and coho salmon of Lake Ontario, Lake Champlain's landlocks average about four pounds during the fall spawning run, with a few fish over ten pounds. Similarly, Lake Champlain's steelhead range from 16 to 20 inches, with some larger specimens over four pounds. Another key difference between Lake Ontario's Pacific salmon and Lake Champlain's landlocks is that landlocked salmon do not die after spawning but return to the lake to feed, grow larger, and then spawn again. For this reason, catching salmon by snagging or lifting is strictly prohibited on the Saranac. (Anglers should consult the NYS Fishing Regulations Guide to learn the special regulations in effect on the lower Saranac.) Although it will never offer salmon that match in either size or number the Pacific salmon that ascend Lake Ontario's Salmon River each fall, the Saranac offers a qualitatively different angling experience more akin to traditional Atlantic salmon fishing. And the landlocks are no less spectacular fighters than their sea-going cousins.

The Saranac's spring salmon run usually begins in early April and continues through mid May, depending on the water temperature and level. The best fishing occurs from the river's mouth to perhaps a half-mile upstream. Although not particularly large at this time of year, averaging between 16 and 20 inches, the salmon are voracious feeders and will hit worms, spoons, plugs, streamers, nymphs and even dry flies. More important than what to use is the task of getting your lure, bait or fly down near the bottom in the swift, heavy waters. Fly fishing anglers should come equipped· with at least a seven weight rod system, and either a full sinking or fast-sink-tip line. Spin and bait anglers would do well to use a long sturdy rod and reel with a dependable drag. Six to eight pound test line will normally handle the most challenging fish.

Early September marks the beginning of the fall spawning migration, with the peak coming by mid October. The salmon ascend the river as far as the Imperial Mill dam three miles upstream. The fish are both larger and more tempermental than in the spring because they are not actively feeding. Patience, in the form of repetitive casts into likely pools and runs, is the only sure way to maximize chances for success. When the salmon are inclined to hit, they will strike almost anything. Worms and plugs continue to work, although fly fishing is perhaps more common in fall. Some anglers have luck using traditional Atlantic salmon flies, with the Cosseboom and Rusty Rat being notable favorites. The majority of fly fishing enthusiasts use streamers and bucktails. Yellow maribou streamers, Grey Ghosts, and Muddlers, in sizes two through eight, are popular patterns. Again, however, the exact pattern seems less important than the mood of the fish at any given moment.

Since the lower Saranac flows directly through the city of Plattsburgh, access is not a problem. Following Route 3 or Route 9 into the downtown section will lead to the mouth of the river and to the city's Verdantique Park along its banks. Ample parking is available, and there is access for handicapped anglers as well. A small trailer launch facility can be found near the city's municipal treatment plant. In the years to come the city plans to extend the Verdantique Park upstream to the Imperial dam, providing additional fishing access points along the way. For the present, however, access to the Imperial pool and to other productive stretches is gained either by parking in back of the college fieldhouse and walking down to the river, or by taking George Angell Drive to the footbridge in back of the Plattsburgh High School. Both areas are located off Rugar Street near the SUNY Plattsburgh campus. Fall fishing can be quite congested at times and will remain so until the construction of fish ladders opens up more water and distributes the pressure.

For all the excitement that surrounds the Saranac's salmon run, anglers should still never be too sure about what they'll catch when they give it a try. Steelhead, smallmouth, walleye, northerns, brown trout and even lakers swim in the same water as the migrant landlocks. And, they hit just often enough to remind everyone of the truth of the proposition that, when fishing the mighty Saranac, it's always best to "expect the unexpected!"

John Spissinger is a trout bum of the first order. John lives in Peru, NY, and has served as secretary and most recently as Regional Director of Trout Unlimited. An ardent fly tier, John has taught flytying classes for the past eight years for Trout Unlimited members in the Plattsburgh area.

5

THE LEGENDARY
AUSABLE

by Francis Betters

A book on fishing in the Adirondacks must include a chapter on the fabled West Branch of The Ausable River, which emanates from the highest peaks in the Adirondacks and, after joining the river's other main branch, flows eventually into Lake Champlain. The 30-mile-long West Branch is considered by many top outdoor writers and a multitude of fishermen who have visited it to be one of the best trout streams in the East. Man with all his wisdom and technical skill could not have drawn a better blueprint for the perfect trout stream than Mother Nature has provided in the West Branch of the Ausable.

The Ausable River consists of two main branches, but it is the West Branch that has received the most attention and rightfully so. It is this branch to which thousands of fly and spin fishermen from all over the United States and many foreign countries come, to try their luck at hooking one of the lunker brown trout that inhabit the many deep pools found here.

To understand why the West Branch is so good, it is important to know what ingredients go into producing a premier trout stream. This in turn necessitates knowing what the trout's requirements are — what it takes to ensure an abundant and healthy population of fish. To sum these requirements up briefly: (1) clean, unpolluted water, (2) a proper temperature range and a good supply of oxygen, (3) a plentiful food supply, and (4) cover.

How does the West Branch stack up in each of these four categories?

The water is still very clean in spite of increasing development in the area, and there are no great pollution problems menacing the river. The rich mineral water from the mountain feeder streams and the rich soil that is found along parts of the West Branch provide a good foundation for the food chains that eventually feed the trout. The river provides good nourishment for both of the major sources of food the trout feed on, namely insects and baitfish.

Traversing a very cold part of the Adirondacks, the West Branch usually runs in a very favorable temperature range for the trout. The shady conditions brought on by steep gorges and overhanging foliage help out in this regard so that even in summer the West Branch is often surprisingly chilly. As for the oxygen content, it is very good, thanks in part to the steep gradient. An abundant supply of oxygen is infused into the river as the water tumbles over the millions of rocks and boulders that make up the stream bottom in a large part of the West Branch.

The lower forms of life that the trout feed on are found in large numbers. The Ausable has an abundance of all three of the most important species of insects: mayflies, stoneflies and caddisflies. These insects are a good source of protein and their abundance promotes good trout growth.

Finally, in regard to requirement number four, cover, the West Branch is hard to beat. Not only are there many deep pools, but there are a multitude of hiding and holding spots created by rocks and boulders and, in places, undercut banks.

It might be added here that another virtue of the Ausable is its very remoteness. It is far from any of the major cities of the east, and this has so far prevented overuse. Also, it is one of the most heavily stocked rivers in New York State.

The West Branch begins its infancy stage in the mountains. The

Fishing the pocket water on one of the prime sections of the West Branch, several miles north of Lake Placid along Rt. 86.

headwaters comprise several brooks which flow essentially north from the Mt. Marcy High Peaks area. As these tumbling mountain brooks converge, they gather strength and at the junction of Marcy Brook and South Meadow Brook the West Branch is officially born. This is at the western edge of the South Meadows area, and just south of the village of Lake Placid. The West Branch then winds its way down past the Olympic ski jumps just outside Lake Placid, picking up Indian Pass Brook on the way.

For the next four or five miles the river is fairly calm as it makes its way through more meadowland, picking up a number of other small feeder streams. This is the part I refer to as the "Sweetwater" section of the Ausable. The river continues to grow, reaching the Rt. 86 bridge about three miles north of Lake Placid. After this crossing, the river really begins to gain character, passing through its rebellious and energetic teenage stage, if you will. A few miles farther downstream, ancient glaciers have carved out a series of deep gorges in what is now called Wilmington Notch. As it tumbles through these gorges, the river takes on the personality by which it is chiefly known. The rocky West Branch is extremely scenic here,

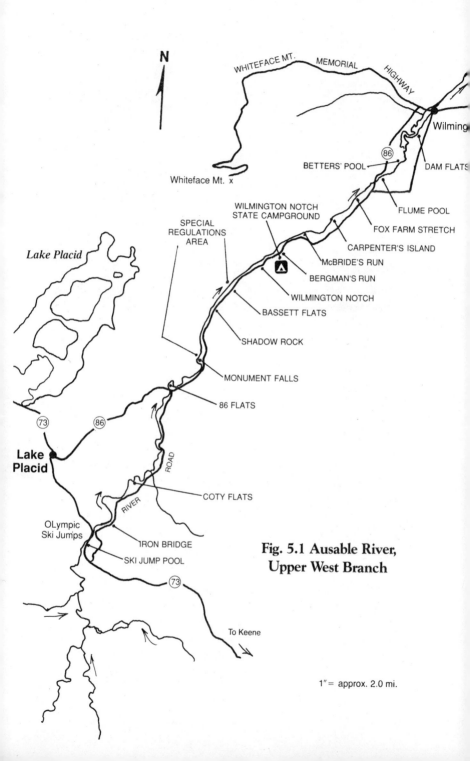

Fig. 5.1 Ausable River, Upper West Branch

1" = approx. 2.0 mi.

with one of the most dramatic spots being about a mile upstream of the Wilmington Notch State Campground. Here, the river roars over a falls that is more than 100 feet in height. Through the millennia, the countless billions of gallons of water churning over this great falls (called High Falls) have gouged out a deep pool within which large trout can hide amid the boulders and ledges. The trout here are comparatively safe from both anglers and from the large chunks of ice that come crashing down each spring when the ice breaks up from the slower sections of river upstream.

For the next two miles, the river sort of catches its breath as it forms numerous pools and pockets before taking another spectacular plunge over another series of falls known today as "The Flume." Beneath this falls, there is another large, deep pool that has become famous over the years and where big trout are taken each spring after ice-out. There is rarely a day during the open trout season when there aren't fishermen lining the ledges along both sides of this famous pool. Surprisingly, in spite of the pressure most of them catch some fish. Over the years, I have taken many good trout in the 15-20 inch range and can recall a half dozen or more lunkers that weighed from four to seven pounds. My largest was a 7¼ pound brown taken on a Hornberg streamer.

About a mile below the Flume Falls, the river seems to rest after its arduous journey and it flows now in a more peaceful fashion until it eventually meets the constraint of a dam located in the center of Wilmington. This is what most of the old-time residents of the village refer to as Lake Everest, but it is merely a dammed up section of stream about two miles long, a hundred to four hundred feet wide and with depths to about twenty feet. This beat of the West Branch holds some lunkers and each spring one or two very large trout are bested by lucky anglers fishing the local beach. Recently, for example, an 8½ pounder was taken by one of the local residents. This two mile section of slow water above the dam is an ideal spot for bait fishermen, but aside from the section between the bridge in town and the dam, and the small beach section, it must be fished from a small boat.

Beneath this dam at Wilmington, another large pool measuring

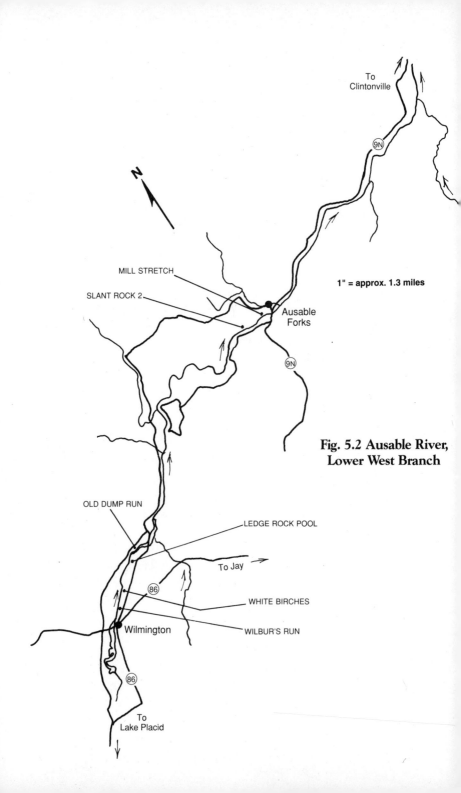

To
Clintonville

9N

N

MILL STRETCH

SLANT ROCK 2

1" = approx. 1.3 miles

Ausable
Forks

9N

Fig. 5.2 Ausable River,
Lower West Branch

OLD DUMP RUN

LEDGE ROCK POOL

To Jay

86

WHITE BIRCHES

Wilmington

WILBUR'S RUN

86

To
Lake Placid

some 400 feet across holds a great many trout, with some over three pounds. A fairly adept fly fisherman can wade out near the center of the stream below the pool and cast up towards the dam. It is an ideal place to fish large streamers and weighted nymphs. It's also a good spot to try big dry flies just before dark, and in the spring after ice-out it is one of the favorite pools of bait fishermen.

The section of stream from the Wilmington dam downstream about two miles is my favorite stretch for fly fishing. Here there are too-numerous-to-count pools and pockets formed by converging currents around boulders, and these create excellent fly fishing water. Access here is difficult, however.

After the river crosses beneath Lewis Bridge below Wilmington, it is posted for about one and a half miles. Fortunately, this is not one of the better parts of the West Branch. The river here is fairly wide and shallow for the most part, with only a few good holding pools. But from where Black Brook empties into the river at the lower end of the posted water, the river again has an increased number of pools and pockets, and these persist for the next six or seven miles. This beat of river from Black Brook to Ausable Forks is known as "The Bush Country". There are numerous old logging roads where one can reach the river, but for the most part it has to be gotten to by foot. New subdivisions and posting have made access here more and more difficult. As with the dammed-up section at Wilmington, the half-mile impounded part of the West Branch above the dam at Ausable Forks contains many trophy size fish.

For about a mile below this dam at Ausable Forks, the West Branch offers up some excellent pocket water for the fly fisherman. It is, however, one of the roughest sections of the river to wade. Its bottom is littered with segments of old bridges, broken boulders and pieces of cement blasted out when the old pulp mills were destroyed years ago.

Just downstream of the bridge in the center of Ausable Forks the West Branch converges with its sister stream, the East Branch, to form the main Ausable. Although the main branch contains some trout, it is not considered top quality trout water. The river is quite wide and shallow for the most part, and it contains a large number of chubs and shiners. A few good pools can be found farther downstream, but as the river is quite shallow, it heats up during the hot summer months and doesn't produce well. Nonetheless, the Main Stem of the Ausable has its devotees and there are trout to be caught.

Let's now get a little bit more specific about a few of the better sections of the West Branch.

The stretch from the Olympic ski jump outside the village of Lake Placid down to the Rt. 86 bridge is for the most part deep water with undercut banks, some faster currents, and a few pools. It may be that the largest trout in the stream are hiding beneath these undercut banks. The DEC once shocked one of the larger pools in this section and turned up three trout over six pounds apiece. (This same scenario also occurs in the mile long section from the Rt. 86 bridge down to Monument Falls, where the trophy sections begins.) This section is best fished with nymphs, small streamers or large wet flies during the early season months. At this time, bait fishermen can excel on this part of the river. During the warmer summer months, small flies in sizes 18-22 work best. Terrestrials such as ants and grasshoppers can be a good choice during the summer period, too. There is also an excellent trico hatch here in August and September.

From the beginning of the trophy section (discussed below) at Monument Falls all the way down to the Flume, the river is broken water with plenty of pockets and pools. Much of this is wadable fly fishing water, and it is very good. Another of my favorite stretches is the approximately one mile section below the Flume. Here, there are a number of islands below which large pools have been formed. These pools produce good-sized trout each spring and fall. This particular section is about two hundred feet off Rt. 86, just north of the Flume bridge.

For the most part, the West Branch is governed by general statewide trout regulations, i.e. ten trout per day no size limit, with the season running from 4/1 to 9/30. However, there are two special regulations sections. The first is from the Rt. 86 bridge northeast of Lake Placid downstream to the Wilmington Dam. Here you can take ten trout nine inches or larger by any legal method, and the season is year-round. Section two lies within section one. This is the beat from Monument Falls downstream 2.2 miles, usually called the Trophy Section. Within this zone you may keep only three trout 12 inches or larger, and you may use artificial lures only. Again, the season is year-round.

Since the trophy section was initiated some dozen years ago, it has become a very popular part of the river. Although the trout do not average much larger than those in the remainder of the stream, the DEC does stock this section from time to time with some of its large breeders. A couple of years ago, they put in about 800 large rainbows up to eight pounds. During the regular trout season, there is probably at least one large trout taken each week from the trophy section.

The East Branch of the Ausable has its origins in the Ausable Lakes area, southwest of the village of Keene Valley. It flows northward along Rt. 9N past the villages of Keene, Jay and Upper Jay. It is a good trout stream by most standards, but pales alongside the West Branch, in terms of both numbers and size of the trout. The East Branch is relatively shallow, without much character, and during the hot months of July and August does not produce well. It is, though, a much tamer river than the West Branch and therefore much easier to wade. There are some good holding pools and the stream is a good choice for the less adventurous and less aggressive fisherman.

The deeper holding pools and runs are few and far between so you will have to explore a greater section of the stream to find them. One nice stretch is from Keene upstream to Hull's Falls. Unlike the West Branch, the East Branch has few good feeder streams. Styles Brook and Clifford Brook are the only two tributaries big enough to contain fair populations of fish.

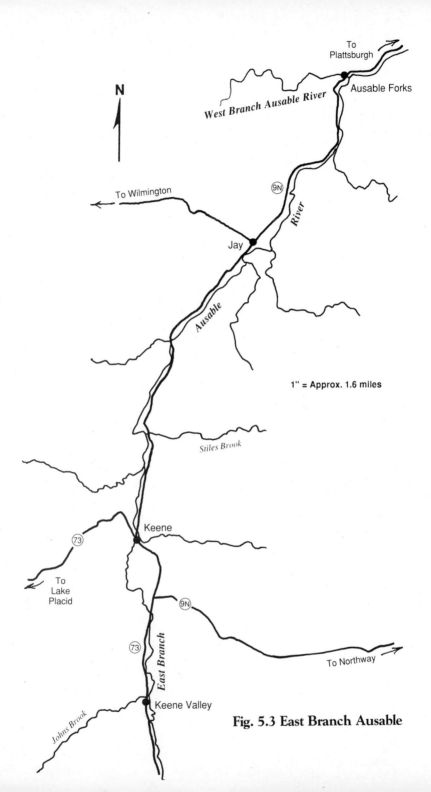

N

To Plattsburgh

Ausable Forks

West Branch Ausable River

9N

River

To Wilmington

Jay

Ausable

1" = Approx. 1.6 miles

Stiles Brook

Keene

73

To Lake Placid

9N

East Branch

73

To Northway

Keene Valley

Johns Brook

Fig. 5.3 East Branch Ausable

The relatively placid East Branch of the Ausable. It has faster sections but it's much tamer than its sister stream to the west.

The West Branch has some larger tributaries that offer excellent fishing. Black Brook, which empties into the river just below the village of Wilmington, is large enough to fly fish and produces a good population of fish. I've taken trout up to four pounds from this brook. Other West Branch tributaries worth mentioning are Beaver Brook (excellent speckled trout fishing) Little Black Brook, Brown Brook and White Brook. All of these tributaries are a mile or less from the village of Wilmington.

Many wonder what the best fishing periods are for the various types of fishing possible on the West Branch. In the spring from April first when the general season opens until about the middle of May is when bait fishermen often do best. The best natural baits are, of course, minnows and worms. In the faster sections of the West Branch, spinners are often the most effective spinning lures. Included here would be Panther Martins, Mepps, Rooster-tails, C.P. or Swiss Swings, etc. In the medium to slower sections, Phoebes and Rapalas are often deadly, but they do not operate as well as spinners in the white water. Fly fishermen during this same early period will do best using small streamers and nymphs fished deep, since the trout are not as active in the cold water and will

be close to the bottom. Good early season patterns are the Grey Ghost, Muddler Minnow, Wooly Worm, and Hornberg.

The best fly fishing months for the dry fly fisherman are May, June, July and September into the middle of October. The first major hatch to emerge is the hendrickson, between the fifth and tenth of May. It is well to remember that the mayfly hatches on the Ausable come off about two weeks later than they do on Catskill streams because of the higher elevation and the colder water temperatures. There are heavy hatches of caddis during May and June and good hatches of stoneflies throughout the season. The longest hatch of the year is the *Isonchyia bicolor,* which comes off beginning around the middle of August and lasts well into October.

Since much of the river is comprised of fast water with many boulders and heavy currents, the most productive flies are usually the larger ones, sizes 10, 12, and 14; smaller flies are often the ticket in the slicks and the pools. The fly that seems to account for more fish than any other is my own Ausable Wulff in sizes 10 and 12. Some of the other especially productive patterns are the dark and light Haystacks, light and dark caddis, Light Cahill, Adams, March Brown and Hendrickson. The most productive nymph patterns are the black, brown and light stonefly nymphs, grey mayfly, all-purpose light, Light Cahill, Hendrickson and blue dun. During July and August, small midges and terrestrials are in order. A good imitation for the *Isonychia* dun is the Dark Haystack with a reddish-brown body.

Another aspect of fishing on the West Branch worth mentioning is the ratio of stocked fish to those spawned in the stream. In the center section of the stream between about Wilmington and the Olympic ski jumps, the trout are mostly stocked fish. A very high percentage of these fish are brown and rainbow trout. From the Olympic ski jump upstream there is a greater percentage of wild speckled trout (in smaller sizes). From the dam in Wilmington downstream you will also find a greater percentage of naturally spawned trout, mostly browns and rainbows, but a fair number of speckled trout as well.

Fly fisherman using a caddis nymph lands a nice brown trout on the Main Stem Ausable below Ausable Forks.

This six or seven mile section from the dam downstream is the most productive water on the river. Here is where you will find the best fly hatches from May through September.

A word of special advice is in order in regard to wading the West Branch of the Ausable. The river has one of the slipperiest bottoms I have ever encountered, thanks to the algae that covers the rocks in many areas of the stream. Combine this with the large and often jagged rocks and you can see why the West Branch is such a treacherous river to wade. It is wise to use both a wading staff and felt-soled waders, or felt soled wading shoes.

Those visiting this region for the first time will find several different types of accommodations. In Wilmington, there are a number of reasonably priced motels. The West Branch Fly Fishing Club has its own motel where fishermen can stay for a modest fee. It's located near the dam in town, right on the best fly fishing section. The lodge has its own lounge with color T.V. and a large kitchen where fishermen can cook their own meals. Although members get first priority on the rooms, other fishermen are given the same rates when rooms are available. For anyone wishing up-to-date stream conditions on the West Branch, there is a local hotline that you can call from April 1st until October 15th. That number is (518) 946-2605.

A more upscale and generally more costly village to stay in is Lake Placid. This scenic site of past Winter Olympiads is admittedly a little bit glitzy, but it does offer a wide range of accommodations and there are some very good restaurants. There is also good transportation (bus, etc.) in and out of Placid.

Many out-of-town anglers who come to fish the Ausable choose a campground as an economical way to spend a few nights. There are a number of choices. One is the Wilmington Notch State Campground, which is located right in the middle of the fishiest section of the river. Another is the Adirondack Loj which offers both indoor lodging and "primitive" outdoor camping. This is located just outside Lake Placid near the South Meadows area, and is administered by the Adirondack Mountain Club (ADK). Private campgrounds are also numerous in the Adirondacks, and can be found in the various campground directories or through chambers of commerce. The West Branch of the Ausable is a river worth traveling to, and indeed, some anglers travel thousands of miles to fish its productive waters. It offers all types of fishing conditions for fishermen of all dispositions, from the timid to the most adventurous.

There is also the nostalgic presence of the many well known anglers who have fished these same waters over the years. Bergman's Run, just upstream of the Flume Pool is named after Ray Bergman. Ray did much of his research for his book *Trout* here on the Ausable. He often fished this section of stream with my Dad and I learned much of my fly tying technique from this quiet and humble man. "Frustration Pool" located above the trophy section was named by another good friend and fellow angler, Jim Deren. Jim never missed fishing his favorite pool on his yearly pilgrimages to the Ausable. He fished this pool for the last time only a few months before he passed away.

The scenic beauty of its tumbling currents in the shadow of Whiteface Mountain, its clean unpolluted waters, and its abundance of trout make the West Branch of the Ausable a stream you will want to return to many times.

Fran Betters operates a large sporting goods business on the banks of the Ausable. He is a fly tyer of legend and has authored several now-famous patterns. He ties thousands of flies each year and conducts fly fishing seminars for beginners and experts alike. He has written five books on fishing and numerous magazine and newspaper articles. He is also president of the West Branch Fly Fishing Club. His latest book is Fran Better's Fly Fishing, Fly Tying and Pattern Guide.

6

IN THE HEART
OF THE ADIRONDACKS
by Brian McDonnell

Deep, clear and cold, Lake Placid lies in the heart of the mountains, at the eastern end of a chain of lakes extending west through the famous Saranac Lakes to scenic Tupper Lake. This so-called Tri-Lakes region of Essex and Franklin counties is a four-season angler's paradise. The large lakes covered in this chapter, together with numerous small ponds, rivers, and brooks in the area, present excellent opportunities for fishermen of every taste. Fly fishing purists will be challenged by the landlocked salmon and trout populations, while worm anglers will enjoy the numerous species of panfish readily caught from boats, bridges and shorelines.

LAKE PLACID

Located just outside the 1980 Winter Olympic host village, Lake Placid lies below Whiteface Mountain, the sixth highest of New York's "high peaks." This spring fed, glacial lake with a gravel and boulder strewn bottom and little vegetation, has an average depth of between sixty and one hundred feet around its three

Beautiful Lake Placid as seen from an overlooking peak several miles away. Some of the biggest lake trout in New York swim in this lake.

prominent islands. It is ideal habitat for lake trout, brook trout (speckled trout) and rainbow trout, all of which are found here. There are also healthy populations of smallmouth bass, northern pike and native whitefish.

According to Lake Placid fishing guide Capt. Uwe Dramm, lake trout are best fished early in the spring and again in the fall. Slow trolling with spoons, spinners or lures set well back on a flat line is best for surface fishing. Twenty pounds or better is considered "trophy" size. The official state record lake trout was caught here in late Spring of 1986. The lunker weighed 34 pounds, 8 ounces and was caught on a large spoon trolled deep. Speckled trout are best fished after ice-out on light tackle when the water is still frigid. Small Roostertails, other spinners or spoons produce results. Capt. Dramm recommends that brook trout fishermen utilize long leaders to successfully boat these easily spooked fish. Rainbow trout are plentiful in Lake Placid with many five pound plus trophies available. While all of the trout species present reproduce naturally in the lake or its tributaries, New York State's Department of Environmental Conservation annually supplements the wild rainbow population with an aggressive stocking program. Rainbow trout are best fished when the lake's surface water warms to over 58 degrees Fahrenheit. Slow troll spoons along the eastern shoreline at dusk for best results.

Lake Placid also supports a healthy smallmouth bass population. They are most common over rocky shoals, uprooted 100-foot white pines along shore, and man made structure. Artificials, especially old style wooden plugs and spinnerbaits, work well. Three pound smallmouths are common. Trophy bass up to about six pounds can also be found by the lucky and the skillful. Several large northern pike have also come from the lake including one eighteen pounder caught a few years ago. Whitefish, too, are taken on occasion; they are native to Lake Placid but have been on the decline the last several decades. Sportsmen are encouraged to return whitefish to the lake unharmed.

There is an excellent public boat launch with facilities near the village where lodging, meals, boat rentals, and bait are available. There are also several licensed guides fishing the lake. The New York State Outdoor Guides Association publishes an annual list of its members. Copies of *The Guide to The Guides* are available by writing NYSOGA, P.O. Box 916F Saranac Lake, NY 12983. It is best to inquire early for peak fishing dates.

TUPPER LAKE

Best known for its bass and pike fishing, Tupper Lake also offers quality lake trout and landlocked salmon fishing. The village of Tupper Lake has a long history of involvement in the wood products industry. The lake itself was dammed and enlarged to assist the transport of logs to the mill. The dams created numerous acres of shallow, weedy water and merged Raquette Pond with the main body of Tupper Lake. The expansive, shallow weed beds provide excellent habitat for northern pike, walleyes, and bass. Live bait is customarily used, though white and chartreuse spinnerbaits have grown in popularity in recent years.

The main body of the original lake stretches from Watch Island to the South Bay, where the Bog River, or Round Pond Outlet, emp-

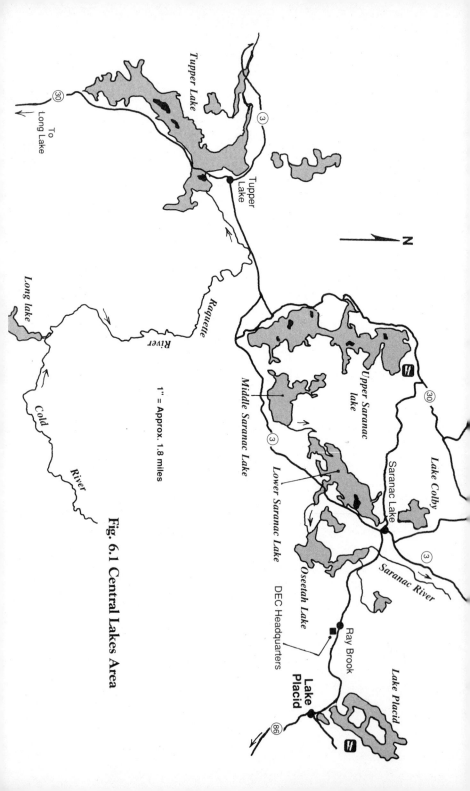

Fig. 6.1 Central Lakes Area

1" = Approx. 1.8 miles

N

Tupper Lake

Tupper Lake

To Long Lake

30

3

Raquette River

Long lake

Cold River

Middle Saranac Lake

Upper Saranac lake

Lower Saranac Lake

30

Saranac Lake

Lake Colby

3

Saranac River

Oseetah Lake

DEC Headquarters

Ray Brook

Lake Placid

Lake Placid

86

ties into the lake in grand fashion over Bog River Falls. The numerous rocky islands and weedy shallow bays offer the bass angler
a variety of fishing locations. Consistent, healthy catches have
increased the popularity of the lake among both locals and visiting anglers.

Though Tupper Lake is best known for its cool water species,
anglers, taken by the scenery and pristine beauty of the lake,
have discovered a well kept "local secret" — lake trout and landlocked salmon. The deeper water between Norway Island and
Black Point offers a challenging alternative to the normal Tupper
Lake regimen. A word of caution: your day of fishing is best
planned for early morning or late afternoon as the prevailing
winds blow up the lake on most days.

There is a state maintained boat launch on Route 30 south of
Tupper Lake village. Lodging, restaurants, boat rentals and live
bait are available in the village and around the lake.

LOWER SARANAC LAKE

Located just west of the village of Saranac Lake, the Saranac
River connects Lower Saranac Lake to Middle Saranac Lake in
the Southwest and to Oseetah Lake, Kiwassa Lake and Lake Flower in the East. The state maintains two sets of locks to allow boat
travel among these picturesque bodies of water. Fishermen can
find tackle shops, live bait, groceries and a wide variety of restaurants and accommodations for all tastes and budgets. Contact
the Saranac Lake Area Chamber of Commerce, 30 Main St.
Saranac Lake, NY 12983 for more information. Campers can
choose from among several area campgrounds or decide to take
up residence on one of the many island campsites maintained by
DEC in Lower Saranac Lake. You will need a boat, and rentals
are available at several locations around the lakes.

Access to the middle and lower lakes and the chain going into
Saranac Lake village can be made through the state maintained
boat ramps on either Lake Flower in Saranac Lake or at First
Pond, by the state bridge three miles west of Saranac Lake on

Route 3. There are several large private boat ramps, and the state maintains canoe and small boat launches at Ampersand Bay on Lower Saranac Lake and on Route 3 at South Creek leading into Middle Saranac Lake.

The predominant sport fishing species in the chain of lakes leading from Lake Flower to Middle Saranac Lake are bass and northern pike. The numerous islands, expansive weed beds and shallow, stumpy former farm lands created by the dam on Lake Flower provide excellent habitat and great fishing. Bass in the one to three pound range are common, while the occasional five-pound plus fish has been known to take a popping plug, golden shiner, spinnerbait, purple worm or crayfish. Northern pike are vicious predators, thus a heavier weight line and a steel leader are recommended for best results. Pike are very opportunistic, and often prey on wounded fish, so live bait or a lure resembling a perch or sucker are most effective. Three to five pound northerns are common while a ten-plus-pounder will give you all the fight you can handle.

There are numerous good fishing spots on each of the lakes. Concentrate on bass around the islands, rocky shoreline and prominent structures like felled trees or docks in the early morning and evening. Locally known hot spots on Lower Saranac Lake include Ampersand Bay, Crescent Bay and the Narrows. Pike can be found in the shallow, weedy bays almost anytime. Early morning near the mouth of the Saranac River at the far end of the lake, or evenings at the mouth of Fish Creek are best bets.

Lake Flower, near the village, is a popular fishing spot for both village residents and summer visitors. Bass and panfish are the primary catches. Oseetah Lake is shallow, stumpy, and loaded with weed beds. Northern pike are plentiful. You may have an opportunity to enjoy competing with an osprey, as they have been known to skim the surface, hook trophy size fish in their talons and return to the top of an old dead pine for dinner.

Kiwassa Lake is tucked away up a channel east of Oseetah Lake. Good sized pike are caught as they move up the waterway on their way to feed in the lake. The spring bass fishing here using popping plugs is excellent.

The Lower Lake is best known for bass, while the fisherman interested in northern pike will head for Middle Saranac (or Round Lake, as it is known locally). Here, fishermen use spinnerbaits around the islands and tease the northerns out of the shallows of the western shoreline by trolling plugs behind a steel leader. A special place for lunch and good fishing hidden up a navigable waterway off the northern bay of Middle Saranac Lake is Weller Pond. In all of the lakes, the best fishing is in the spring and fall, but quality catches are at times enjoyed even on the hottest days of the summer. Not to be overlooked in the tri-lakes area is ice fishing. The ice angler can enjoy some truly fine hard water fishing in the area. One spot is in Lower Saranac Lake, where an angler can fill his bucket with the large numbers of smelt and yellow perch that winter in the shallow coves and weed beds of the lower lake.

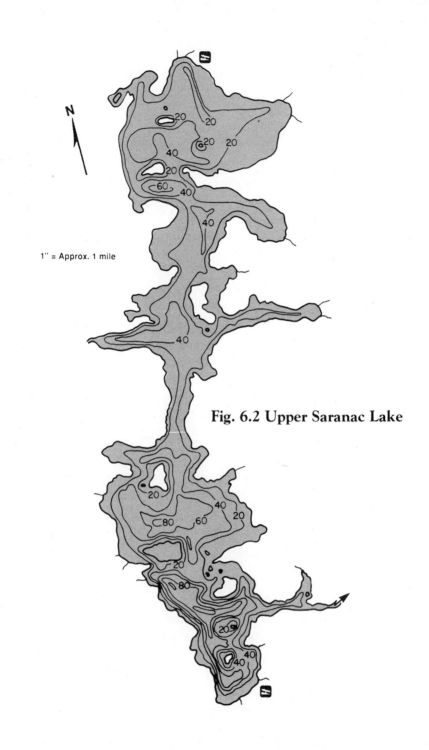

1" = Approx. 1 mile

Fig. 6.2 Upper Saranac Lake

LAKE COLBY AND UPPER SARANAC

Near Lower Saranac Lake, on Route 86, Lake Colby is another fine example of a year-round fisherman's paradise. In winter a virtual shanty town appears, as ice fishermen establish themselves over their favorite holes. Species sought include rainbow and brown trout, as well as kokanee salmon, smelt, splake, and perch. The unofficial close of the ice fishing season is the annual ice fishing derby sponsored by the Saranac Lake Fish and Game Club held the first weekend of March. There are numerous cash and merchandise awards for winners in several categories.

When the ice goes out on Lake Colby the fish shanties may disappear, but the fishermen do not. Canoe and small boat access is available at the DEC maintained boat launch on Route 86 across from the General Hospital of Saranac Lake. Brown trout and splake are caught by patient springtime anglers trolling the length of the lake, from the beach to the state boat launch site and up the shore in front of DEC's Camp Colby Environmental Education Camp. Rainbows are sought by summertime fishermen trolling slowly around the middle of the lake, especially off the point past the former Camp Intermission. Bass fishermen have also discovered the shallows of the western bays of this year-round fishing hole.

Upper Saranac Lake is the largest in the chain, stretching seven miles from the state maintained boat ramp at the site of the historic Saranac Inn to the small boat launching site at the end of Indian Carry off Route 3. Some of the deepest water in the Adirondacks, eighty to one hundred feet, is found in the area between Chapel Island and the Wawbeek Resort at the southern end of the lake. This deep water annually attracts lake trout fishermen to the upper lake, who anticipate the time when the lakers will be rolling on the water's surface and the chances will be best for landing a trophy fish. A second cold water gamefish, the landlocked salmon, has also become popular among upper lake fishermen. Early June fly rod trolling with lead core lines and large streamers is effective. As the summer weather forces the fish deeper, downriggers are useful in getting the lure to the fish.

The Saranac between Lakes Flower and Oseetah. Mt. McKenzie is in the background.

The rocky, shallow coves and several large islands of Upper Saranac Lake offer anglers a complete change of tackle from that normally used for lakers or salmon. Smallmouth and rock bass are popular summertime species as are northern pike in the shallow bays of the northern end of the lake. Live bait and spinnerbaits work best in Saginaw or Square Bays.

Adding to the diversity of the lake is the ice fishing that can be enjoyed for smelt and yellow perch on any of the bays accessible from State Route 30 along the western shore of the lake.

Fishermen concentrating on the upper lake can find campsites, groceries and supplies at Fish Creek on Route 30. Comfortable accommodations and meals are also available a short walk from the lake.

Another nighttime fishing activity popular with area residents and visiting campers is the pursuit of bullheads. Bullheads are a bottom dwelling species present in every lake in the Saranac chain. Nightcrawlers, a bobber, a lamp or fire, and a few good friends are all you need for a good night of bullheading.

The diverse opportunities for fishing in the Tri-Lakes and surrounding waterways provide the angler with numerous options within a half hour drive of a motel room, campsite, or summer home. Cold water species like lake trout, landlocked salmon, browns, rainbows and splake; cool water species like bass and northern pike; good eating panfish like perch, rock bass and sunfish; plus social fishing for bullheads in the spring and summer and smelt and perch in the winter — all this combines to make the Tri-Lakes Region a four season fisherman's paradise.

Brian McDonnell is a New York State licensed guide, and is past president of the New York State Outdoor Guides Association. He is also the NYS representative to the Professional Guide's Association. Brian owns McDonnell's Adirondack Challenges, a guide service and canoe rental business located in Saranac Lake. He leads fishing, canoeing, hiking, cross country skiing and snowshoeing trips in the central Adirondacks and beyond.

BACKPACKING
FOR TROUT
by Jim Gould

The complete wilderness experience awaits you when you begin to explore the angling challenges that lie beyond the roadside and the marked trail. The Adirondacks offer myriad backcountry trout fishing adventures, whose itinerary can include climbing an Adirondack peak and bushwhacking to a remote pond in addition to spending mornings casting flies to small stream brook trout. With some specialized equipment, a little extra preparation, and a good measure of curiosity, you can have brook trout in your frying pan at every evening's campfire.

First, you will need to inventory your backcountry skills as well as your outdoor equipment. Though the beauty of the Adirondacks is alluring, the potential for a life threatening experience is very real. The ability to use a compass and read a topographical map is essential, even in an area with marked trails. Bushwhacking (hiking without the aid of a trail) will also increase your angling possibilities significantly.

The weather in the mountains is unpredictable, with hypothermia a possibility even in the summer months. Bringing rain gear (rainproof, not rain-resistant) is mandatory, as is wearing an assortment of wool and/or breathable synthetic clothing. Cotton loses nearly all of its insulating qualities when wet, so avoid all-cotton attire, especially in the spring and autumn when nighttime temperatures typically fall below freezing. The same principle applies to natural fiber sleeping bags. Down-filled bags lose their warmth once wet, so a synthetic, fiber-filled bag rated to at least 20 F. is strongly suggested.

Though many of the wilderness areas we'll describe here offer lean-tos, a lightweight tent or tarp will allow you the freedom to choose your own campsite. Just be sure to make camp 150 feet from any water source or trail, as per New York State Department of Environmental Conservation (DEC) guidelines.

As wild and pure as backcountry wilderness areas may seem, assume the water is unsafe for drinking until purified. Giardia, a microorganism often present in mountain water sources, can cause severe vomiting and diarrhea. Known locally as "beaver fever," giardia is a cyst spread through the feces of many mammals, including humans. To make water potable, bring it to a rolling boil for ten minutes. Higher altitudes and cold temperatures may require a longer boiling time. Another alternative is chemical purification tablets, but they will alter the flavor of the water. A recent and affordable innovation is a small filter-pump, the "First Need Water Purifier," which weighs less than a pound and screens out most microorganisms. To ensure a clean water supply, bury human waste at a depth of six inches and a distance of at least 150 feet from any water supply. The same rule goes for washing of any sort — keep clear of streams or ponds and use biodegradable soap.

Open fires, if controlled and employed at an established campsite, are permitted in Adirondack wilderness areas. A small backpacking stove, though, can provide a consistent cook source wherever you may be even when wood is wet or scarce. Don't forget waterproof matches, a small first-aid kit, and a flashlight with new batteries.

To lighten your load, you may want to pack prepared, freeze-dried meals, which have become tastier and more nutritious in the last decade. Remember to carry along the ingredients for your favorite fish preparation recipe. Whatever you decide to pack, take the DEC dictum to heart: if you carry it in, carry it out. Leave as little impact on the wilderness as possible.

Though your equipment list may already appear monumental, if you pack economically, stressing lightweight articles, you should expect to carry between forty-five to sixty pounds, depending on your length of stay. At first glance, that weight may appear impractical for hiking to several remote trout ponds; however, if you select a centralized location as your base camp, a place where you are likely to sleep and prepare your meals, your day-trip load will be much lighter and much more manageable for fishing and hiking. Also, since you should travel with a friend for safety reasons, much of your load can be shared. (Be advised that overnight groups of ten or more require a DEC permit.)

With the emphasis on the reduced load, you may have to leave that cumbersome tackle box home. Pick out the essentials — a handful of reliable flies and/or lures — and pack it all in a container the size of this book. It is not uncommon to bring both a fly and spin outfit, or a combo outfit, to be prepared for any conditions. For instance, a very windy day can just about end your dry fly casting, while most spinning outfits can perform even in a stiff breeze. Remember your fillet knife and a small net, but forget about boot-foot waders; their excessive weight negates any advantage they may offer. If you feel you must have waders, use the very lightweight stocking foot waders along with an old pair of sneakers. A lightweight float tube or a small inflatable raft, designed for backpackers and available now from many outfitters, may also offer an alternative to shoreline casting.

Some general bait and tackle rules apply to most brook trout ponds in the Adirondacks. If you're spin fishing, worms, spoons, spinners, or minnow type lures work effectively in early spring or late fall when the colder surface temperatures keep trout deeper. As temperatures increase in late spring so does the trout's metabolism. Now they'll come to the surface consistently, allowing you to use lighter gear and surface lures. Fly anglers often turn to one of four basic dry flies: the Black and White, Red and White, Black Leech, and Lead-Winged Dutchman. Of course, a fly resembling the current hatch will also be effective. Wet flies, nymphs, and streamers are often successful for stratified water conditions, with the Black Prince, Grey Ghost, Black Ghost, and Mickey Finn particularly productive.

State-managed lands make all of this good fishing possible for both residents and non-residents, and with the "Forever Wild" amendment to the state constitution in place, these lands will likely remain undisturbed. But there is one negative force threatening this wilderness: Many high-altitude ponds in the Adirondacks have been devastated by the effects of acid precipitation. Brook trout, although more tolerant of high acidity than many species, have been eliminated in many ponds. Even many of the plant forms that contribute to a healthy ecosystem have been hurt. For further information on this critical environmental issue, see the discussion in the beginning of the book.

In many instances, a canoe can figure in a backpack trout excursion. Well marked and maintained portages make it possible.

For the maximum combination of adventure and relaxation, three days and two nights — an average weekend — is the recommended length of stay for the backcountry trout trips described here.

PHARAOH LAKE WILDERNESS AREA

The Pharaoh Lake Wilderness Area presents an extraordinary number of fishing, hiking, and camping experiences. More than thirty ponds, many of them aerially-stocked by state or county fisheries departments, dot the nearly 41,000-acre mountainous landscape, with well-marked and maintained trails connecting many of these fine brook trout waters. The state-owned and managed Pharaoh Lake Wilderness Area receives approximately 10,000 visitors each year, but much of the recreational use occurs in the fringe areas in and around Putnam Pond Campground and southern Pharaoh Lake. Its convenient location, just off Interstate 87 east of Schroon Lake and west of Ticonderoga, also contributes to its attractiveness.

Crane Pond, one of the largest in the Pharaoh Lake area, is the logical starting point for a multi-day trout trip. It is just inside the area's northwest boundary, with a convenient parking area adjacent to its shores. Because of this area's "wilderness" designation, the Crane Pond parking area and the unimproved road which leads to it are slated for closure by the DEC, but pressure from local politicians has kept it open at this writing. Call the DEC for an up-to-date report before you go. The northeastern end of Crane Pond is excellent for lake trout, especially early in the season. In addition to Crane's all-around fishing — smallmouth bass, northern pike, yellow perch, and landlocked salmon — many scenic and productive brook trout waters are just a few miles into the interior.

For instance, Oxshoe, Horseshoe, and Rock Ponds all have lean-tos or campsites on their shores, making each pond's central location a particularly good base camp for day-trips to the many nearby bodies of water. The trails are well maintained, with large hemlock and white pine dominating the landscape. Bushwhacking also is relatively effortless, as the mature woods, open and tall, allow the topography to be easily read and traversed.

You will be impressed by the extensive beaver activity in this area. Many of the ponds owe their great depths, even their very existence, to the beaver dams found across their outlets. Glidden Marsh, for example, should probably be renamed, as dams have nearly doubled its size since the 1950s to make it more pond-like. You'll pass Glidden Marsh on your right, at about eight miles, as you hike the trail to Oxshoe Pond. As with most of the ponds in this area, Glidden Marsh's waters are restricted to artificial lures only. No bait, live or dead, is allowed.

Oxshoe Pond's deep waters and rocky shore make it ideal for shoreline casting for brook trout. A lean-to sits on a rock ledge at its southwestern end, and well-spaced, unimproved campsites line its perimeter. If you are fly fishing, a Black Leech or black and white fly will bring you luck here. Spin fishermen will do well with spoons.

Although the terrain and distances create an environment unsuited for practical canoe travel, there is an unmarked portage connecting Crane Pond and Oxshoe Pond. Just east of Crane's southernmost bay you will find a very small inlet; a herdpath climbs this low point in the topography for approximately one-half mile to Oxshoe Pond.

Though relatively small, Horseshoe Pond will bring you lots of angling activity. A terrific campsite can be found on its central "peninsula" where plenty of open rock and deep water will keep you busy with surfacing brookies.

Lilypad Pond, to the east of Horseshoe Pond, is attractive for its lean-to and central location, but the tear-shaped pond's shore is marshy and dense. Although challenging, it will yield some hard-won trout.

Rock Pond's scenic beauty is matched by the fertility of its waters. As you approach it from the east on the trail from Lilypad Pond, you will notice a beaver dam which has raised the pond's water level at least three feet. This has caused a few sections of the trail, especially on the northeastern end of the pond, to be flooded out. Still, Rock Pond's shoreline, sculpted with many open rock formations, provides several superb campsites, fishing and swimming holes, and open vistas. A marked trail circles the pond making all vantage points easily accessible. An open rocky point on its westernmost shore is guaranteed to keep the spin fisher active, while the fly angler can cast flies on the productive, shallower waters near the inlet from Little Rock Pond, which is nestled in the woods to the east. A clean lean-to sits back from Rock Pond's eastern shore, giving good privacy but poor immediate fishing access. On the other hand, Little Rock Pond's lean-to stands northeast on a high rock ledge, perfect for deep water casting and excellent views. In addition, the bridge linking the ponds makes for a nice casting platform, ideal for throwing flies to brookies.

Many other excellent angling waters are within proximity of Oxshoe, Horseshoe, and Rock Ponds. Clear Pond and North Pond (actually a northern bay of Putnam Pond) are no more than a mile hike from Rock Pond. Less accessible but very rewarding are Bear Pond in the northeast corner of the wilderness area and Lost Pond on the eastern boundary. Burge Pond, stocked with brookies, and Gooseneck Pond, known locally for its lake trout, are also out of the way but worth the effort. Goose Pond, west of Crane Pond, is well-known for its heavily stocked trout waters — brook, splake, rainbow — but its nearness to the road, only a .5 mile hike, invites heavy use.

Pharaoh Lake, the largest body of water in this area with more than four miles of shoreline, is extremely popular. This heavy use is no doubt due in part to the ten thousand brook trout fingerlings dropped there annually by state fisheries aircraft. Lake trout also thrive in Pharaoh Lake's 100-foot depths, and cool water species such as perch and smallmouth bass can be taken as well. Unimproved campsites abound on the shores, with over fifty currently established. Eight lean-tos also sit among the shoreline hemlock and white pine.

To round out your wilderness experience, a hike up Pharaoh Mountain is a must for any backcountry fishing itinerary. The most popular route departs from Crane Pond on a well-marked trail, passes Glidden Marsh, and reaches the firetower perched on the rocky summit after a three-mile hike and 1,457 feet of ascent. A clear day atop Pharoah Mountain, elevation 2,551 feet, affords a nearly 360-degree vista, with Pharaoh Lake and Vermont's Green Mountains to the east and the Adirondack High Peaks, particularly Giant Mountain, to the west.

The Pharaoh Lake Wilderness Area can be entered from several access points. The Crane Pond parking area and trailhead is just off NY 9, at the end of Crane Pond Road. Take the Northway, Interstate 87, to Exit 28 (Schroon Lake), then turn right (south) on NY 9. Alder Meadow Road will be on your left at .6 miles; make this left. A fork appears in the road at 2.1 miles; bear left here and follow Crane Pond Road 3.3 miles to its terminus at the parking area and trailhead on Crane Pond. Remember to add a 1.9 mile hike to Crane Pond if Crane Pond Road is closed and the new parking area and trailhead are established at the boundary of the wilderness area.

On your right, you'll pass the trailhead to Goose Pond (a .5 mile walk on a marked path), 2.3 miles from the Alder Meadow Road turnoff. From the Crane Pond trailhead, Glidden Marsh is .7 miles, Pharaoh Lake 3.4 miles, Oxshoe Pond 1.4 miles, Horseshoe Pond 2.9 miles, and Rock Pond is 4.8 miles.

An alternative access point, which may be more convenient if Crane Pond Road is eventually closed to vehicular traffic, is on NY 74, west of Eagle Lake. From the junction of the Northway and NY 74 at Exit 28, travel east and the trailhead is on your right (south) at 7.7 miles. From that point, Horseshoe Pond is 4.1 miles, Rock Pond 4.2, Oxshoe Pond 5.4, and Crane Pond is 6.9 miles.

Yet another access point is at the Putnam Pond Campground, which lies on the eastern edge of the wilderness area, just 3.5 miles southwest of Chilson on NY 74. Chilson is 13.2 miles east of the Northway and five miles west of Ticonderoga. From the Putnam

Pond Campground trailhead, Rock Pond is three miles, Horse-shoe Pond (via the southern shore of Rock Pond) 5.4 miles, Oxshoe Pond 6.9 miles, and Pharaoh Lake (via Grizzle Ocean) more than seven miles away.

DEC distributes a map of the Pharaoh Lake Wilderness Area based on the 15-minute topo map, Paradox Lake, and adjacent quadrangles. The DEC map is up to date with trail and lean-to information, but its contour lines can be difficult to read. If you plan to travel off-trail, play it safe and bring the USGS 15- minute topo Paradox Lake or the USGS 7.5-minute Pharaoh Mountain. The new 100,000 series USGS maps are also very useful.

Groceries, camping supplies, and an excellent selection of bait and tackle are available in the villages of Schroon Lake and Ticonderoga.

For a discussion of the history and geology of the Pharaoh Lake region, see Barbara McMartin's *Discover the Eastern Adiron-dacks* (Backcountry Publications, Woodstock, Vermont, 1988).

THE SANTANONI PRESERVE

The historic Santanoni Preserve, part of the more than 226,000-acre High Peaks Wilderness Area, can augment your backcountry trout adventure with mountain views and challenging lake and brook trout fishing.

This 10,000-acre preserve was added to the Adirondack Forest Preserve in 1970 when the Pruyn family donated their example of an Adirondack Great Camp and land to the state of New York. The camp, built in 1888 and one of the earliest and finest examples of Adirondack log architecture in existence, stands on the eastern shore of the principal body of water in the preserve, Newcomb Lake. Similar to other such structures lying on state forest preserve lands, the grounds surrounding the multi-building complex are open to the public while the interiors are officially off-limits.

Another interesting feature of the Santanoni Preserve is the gravel road through the wilderness which connects Newcomb

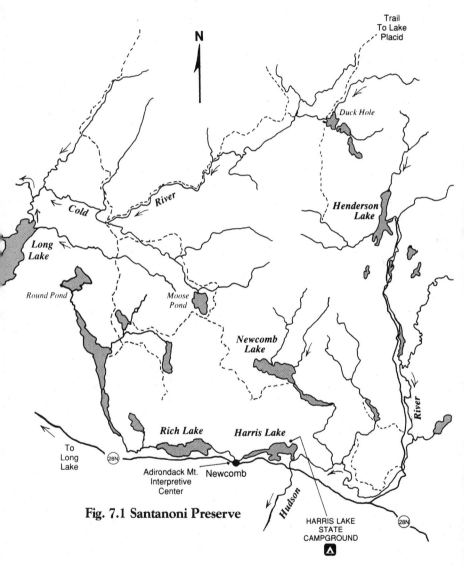

N

Trail
To Lake
Placid

Duck Hole

Cold *River*

Henderson
Lake

Long
Lake

Round Pond

Moose
Pond

Newcomb
Lake

River

Rich Lake   *Harris Lake*

To
Long
Lake

(28N)

Adirondack Mt.   Newcomb
Interpretive
Center

Hudson

(28N)

HARRIS LAKE
STATE
CAMPGROUND

Fig. 7.1 Santanoni Preserve

1" = Approx. 1.9 miles

Lake and Moose Pond with the village of Newcomb, a round-trip distance of between nine and twenty miles depending on your itinerary. Although not open to motorized vehicles of any type, the unimproved road is accessible by other modes of transport. A sturdy bicycle, ideally what is now marketed as a "mountain bike," can carry you and your fishing gear comfortably over the rolling one-lane road. Another option, which may be more practical if you wish to bring in a larger party or canoe, is a horse and wagon service offered by local horsemen. Of course, hiking along this picturesque lane will also get you into the heart of this wilderness, and allow you more freedom to explore.

With several islands and panoramic views, Newcomb Lake's several miles of shoreline offer varied fishing conditions. At the shallower northwestern end of the lake near one of its three inlets, you'll find good brook trout waters as well as lake trout lurking in the cooler depths. A productive trout hole is adjacent to the large boulder known locally as Fish Rock, just off the northwest shore. Two well-placed, state-maintained lean-tos are tucked into the mixed hard and softwoods of that end of Newcomb Lake. A few unimproved campsites can also be found here, and three maintained but shelterless campsites sit nicely in a grove of hemlock and cedar along Upper Duck Hole, the southeastern bay and outlet of the lake. Both Upper Duck Hole, and even Lower Duck Hole to the southeast, are good trout waters, making those campsites conveniently attractive. Colorful waterfowl, including mergansers and buffleheads, can be seen in abundance on these waters.

Hike nearly five miles to the northwest and you'll find Moose Pond and Shaw Pond, which sit at the end of the unimproved road from Newcomb Lake. Moose Pond, the largest of the two with about 2.5 miles of shoreline, is shallow and remote, but that has not deterred many anglers seeking native brook trout there. However, their impact may have significantly depleted Moose Pond's stock. Nevertheless, the rocky southeastern shore may bring you some luck, especially off its tree-covered point. The sandy western shore, while more frustrating to anglers, affords to the northeast a breathtaking view of Santanoni Peak with a distinctive rockslide on the western flank. The Seward Range can also be seen to the north and northeast.

Shaw Pond, east of Moose Pond following an unmarked linking trail, is marshy and shallow, and will be frustrating for shoreline casting. Any trout taken from here will be well-earned.

To round out your wilderness experience, Santanoni Peak can be climbed by bushwhacking along Ermine Brook, an inlet northeast of Moose Pond, and then hiking along the ridge of the Santanoni Range to Santanoni Peak at 4,607 feet. For the very ambitious, Panther Peak, elevation 4,442 feet, is separated from Santanoni Peak by an approximately 1.5 mile herdpath on the ridge. This strenuous climb, requiring competent compass and topographical map reading skills, is recommended only for advanced hikers, as the distance covered one-way is more than three miles from Moose Pond, with an ascent of at least 2,800 feet.

The village of Newcomb is on NY 28N in the heart of the Adirondacks and can be reached from the east via Northway Exits 23, 26, or 29, or from the west via NY 30 coming from Long Lake. Once in Newcomb, turn north at the DEC sign, "Santanoni Preserve." Follow that road for one-third of a mile where you'll find the original gatehouse to the Santanoni Camp, a DEC parking area, and the trailhead.

After registering at the trailhead, proceed down the unimproved road for two miles to a junction. To the right (east) at 2.7 miles lies Santanoni Camp and Newcomb Lake, and to the left (north), at approximately 4.5 miles, are Moose and Shaw Ponds. The trail to the lean-tos on the western shore of Newcomb Lake leaves from the north side of the unimproved road nearly two miles from this junction.

A round-trip visit of both Newcomb Lake and Moose Pond along the unimproved roads, which will involve some backtracking, covers more than 20 miles, and remember to add more for the numerous spur trails around each body of water. Allow

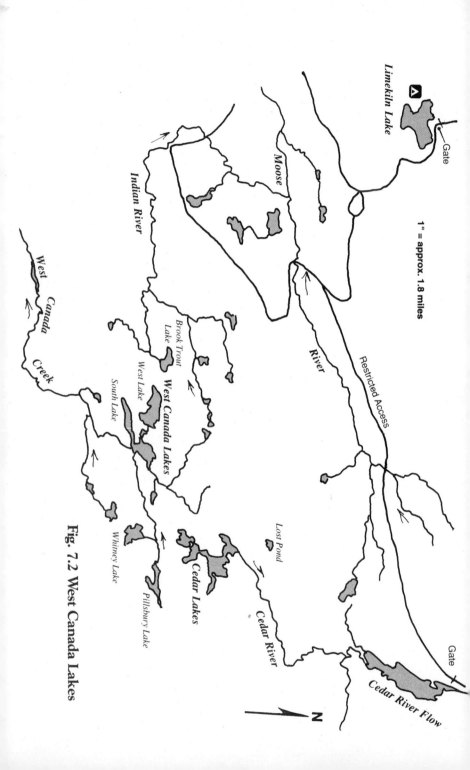

Fig. 7.2 West Canada Lakes

four hours traveling time by bicycle or horse and wagon; triple that time if traveling by foot. Horse and wagon operators can be contacted through the Village Clerk in Newcomb. Day rates range from $35 to $50, depending on group size, cargo, and destination. Reservations at least a week in advance are almost always required. Groceries and a small selection of bait and tackle are available in Newcomb.

The USGS 7.5-minute quadrangle designated Santanoni Peak, is strongly recommended, though it doesn't give an accurate description of the unimproved roads in this area. You'll have to go to the map, "Trails of the Adirondack High Peak Region," published by the Adirondack Mountain Club (Glens Falls, New York) for that important information. For more information on Camp Santanoni, see Harvey H. Kaiser's *Great Camps of the Adirondacks* (Godine, Boston, 1982).

OTHER BACKPACK ADVENTURES

The Adirondacks are a brook trout aficionado's delight. Yet one more is the West Canada Lakes Wilderness Area, which is traversed by the historic 132-mile Northville-Placid Trail. Beaver Pond and the southernmost West Canada Lake (South Lake) are within relatively easy distance from the hiking trail. To reach the interior of this primitive area, take the Cedar River Road west from Indian Lake, park your car and you will be within a day's hike from good fishing and camping.

Other remote wilderness areas with plenty of backcountry trout opportunities are the Siamese Ponds Wilderness Area, which is five miles west of North Creek (Warren County) on NY 28, and the Five Ponds Wilderness Area, located 15 miles northeast of Old Forge (Herkimer County) on NY 28 (see Ch. 15). Contact DEC for maps and access information.

With more than 2,500 ponds and lakes in the Adirondacks, plus endless miles of streams, your passion for the brook trout and for the solitude and wild beauty of its domain will continually be nurtured. The few spots we've just discussed are only a starting point. Follow your nose and a new angling adventure can be found just over the next hill, through the trees, on an enchanting Adirondack pond.

Jim Gould is a professor of English at Paul Smiths College in the heart of the Adirondacks. He writes both fiction and non-fiction, and his work has appeared in numerous publications, including the New York Times, Adirondack Life, Environment *and others.*

8

QUIET STREAMS AND
A PEACEFUL LAKE

by Val De Cesare

Cradled at the foot of Pharaoh Mountain is a nine-mile-long lake that offers visitors a panoramic view of the Adirondack Mountains. Its north-south axis parallels U.S. Rt. 9 between Exits 26 and 28 of the Northway. Schroon Lake begins at a point some five miles north of Chestertown and extends to one mile north of Schroon Lake village. Northbound motorists should get off at Exit 26 from I-87 and head north on Rt. 9 while those southbound should use Exit 28 and head south on Rt. 9.

Schroon is a very pretty lake, with deep blue waters. It has a surface area of 4,230 acres and a maximum depth of 152 feet. Although it is about nine miles long it is not very wide. The widest point, off Adirondack village at the southern end, is about 1½ miles. Year-round fishing is permitted for most species, though northern pike is closed between March 15 and May I. You may use up to five tip-ups and two hand jigs in winter.

There are two public boat launches on Schroon Lake. One is in the village of Schroon Lake and is free. The other is in the town of Horicon at the southern tip of Schroon Lake. This is a state owned boat launch site, and is also free. There is a marina at the northern tip of the lake that will accomodate all of your boating needs. You may also moor your boat there between fishing trips.

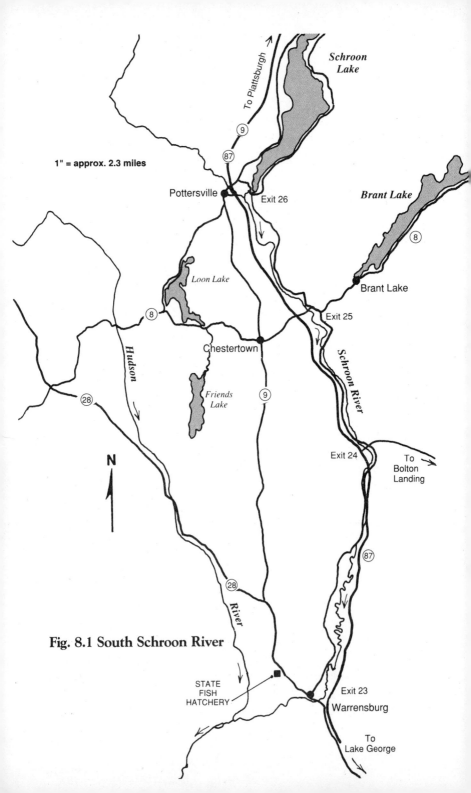

1" = approx. 2.3 miles

Schroon Lake

To Plattsburgh

Brant Lake

Pottersville

Exit 26

Loon Lake

Brant Lake

Exit 25

Schroon River

Chestertown

Friends Lake

Exit 24

To Bolton Landing

Hudson

N

River

Fig. 8.1 South Schroon River

STATE FISH HATCHERY

Exit 23

Warrensburg

To Lake George

Schroon Lake is noted for its landlocked salmon, and has always supported a natural population of this species. Lately, the Department of Environmental Conservation has been conducting an intensive program to bolster salmon numbers. The best time to fish for landlocks is early spring when the fish are near or at the surface feeding on the smelt that congregate near the mouths of streams at this time.

In the spring, I prefer to fish with a small boat and motor, trolling the areas out from the mouth of the Schroon River or other small tributaries. The most popular locations are the entire north end of the lake above Sola Bella Island, and south of the Schroon River. During periods of high water, this whole portion may be trolled, including the river itself. Water depth may restrict you at other times.

Most of the local fishermen prefer to troll streamer flies, Rapalas and Mooselook Wobblers. Rapalas should be trolled at about $3\frac{1}{2}$ miles per hour while Mooselooks are trolled between $3\frac{1}{2}$ and $4\frac{1}{2}$ miles per hour. Streamer flies are trolled rather fast, and they must be jerked periodically to give them a fish-like appearance as they are pulled through the water.

The Sebago Smelt and the Grey Ghost are probably the most used streamer patterns. Other colors and patterns may be used, but you must remember that you are trying to imitate smelt. A number 7 Rapala in either silver or gold is my favorite. Give the Countdown Rapala a try when the surface water is extremely cold. This lure trolls a little deeper and may help you connect. My favorite colors for Mooselooks are white/red dots and orange/black dots.

Summer fishing for landlocks is a completely different story. The lures, for the most part, must be kept at or near the thermocline. This requires more sophisticated equipment and hiring a guide might be the best strategy for a novice. Those having the proper equipment may use the same lures and speeds recommended for spring surface trolling. Downriggers are the most efficient way of getting your lure to the thermocline, but you may use lead core line too. You'll have to experiment with just how much line to let out. The weight of your line and the speed you move at will determine how deep your lure runs.

Trolling for lake trout probably is best from late May to the middle of July. Techniques for lake trout differ greatly from those used for landlock salmon, though. Trolling along the bottom and at slower speeds is recommended. Some people prefer copper trolling line to bring their lure to the bottom while others prefer lead core line or steel line with or without a sinker to hold bottom. Lures for lake trout include those used for salmon plus many other local favorites. Skinny Hinckleys, Suttons, and Leatherstocking are just a few. It has traditionally been best to troll in water that is thirty to eighty feet deep. (Very few fish are ever caught in water over eighty feet.) I prefer water that is between forty and eighty feet deep.

One of the local favorite spots to fish lake trout is the area immediately west of Sola Bella Island. Troll basically north-south about 200 yards west of the island, principally covering the southern half of the island. Then head from the southern tip of the island west towards Grove Point. By the way, Solla Bella Island is also known as Clark's Island and Word of Life Island. Another favorite spot for forktails is the easterly shore of the narrows. This water is approximately sixty to eighty feet deep.

Probably the most productive area for lunker lakers is in the southern half of the lake. There is a sunken island between Adirondack village and Scaroon Manor which is always well marked with buoys. Try all around this spot, especially where the water is fifty to eighty feet deep (which is primarily north and west of Sunken Island). There is an eighty foot channel that runs north-south between Scaroon Manor and Eagle Point. Fish the shallower portions of this channel early in the year and then go deeper as the water warms.

Another good laker spot runs from Adirondack village north towards the Narrows. This area is very uneven in depth and not very well defined as to direction. If you want, just try to hold to about a fifty foot depth. Don't worry if your depth varies. Going south from Adirondack village along the east shore, I would hold between fifty and eighty feet.

Ice fishing is extremely popular on Schroon Lake. Northern pike is only one of several species that make braving the cold worthwhile.

In the fall, as the surface temperature drops to approximately fifty-five degrees, salmon and lake trout may again be caught on the surface. Use the same techniques and lures as for spring fishing for these species.

Fishing through the ice is probably the most effective way to land lunker lake trout and salmon. Schroon lake and most of the surrounding ponds freeze up solid by about the 20th of December, give or take ten days.

Fowler Avenue and Dock Street provide two excellent access points for the ice fisherman to the northern portion of Schroon Lake. Just out from Fowler Avenue on the west shore is a good drop-off for lakers and salmon. Dock Street usually provides good vehicular access to the whole northern basin. Again, the area west of the island is excellent. Another good spot is the eastern shore below the island. Shanties are usually very much in evidence over the better locations. (The bait shop in Schroon Lake village rents shanties.) The central portion of the lake is probably best in the general vicinity of the Narrows. Access to this area can be made via Hayes Road off Rt. 9, or over the bank by the Narrows Restaurant.

About a mile south of Exit 27 (northbound only) off I-87 is Eagle Point Campsite. Just north and south of the campsite along the eastern shoreline is another good area to fish. Access is obtained through the campsite or by parking farther south and walking out onto the lake.

Continuing south along Rt. 9 and just north of the town of Pottersville we take a right onto River Road. Cross the Schroon River bridge and pass the state boat launch at Horicon then go left onto East Shore Road. Approximately four miles to the north you will see the village of Adirondack where Mill Brook enters Schroon Lake. This is a good access point to fish the east shore of the southern basin. Fish fairly close to shore to the south and go farther away from shore to the north. Again, there should be some shanties out to guide you as to where to go.

Live smelt suspended about ten to fifteen feet below the ice seem to produce the most fish, but dead smelt are sometimes just as effective. (Smelt may be purchased at the local bait stores.) I like to stay in waters that are between thirty and sixty feet deep, but I have seen fish caught in waters up to eighty and one hundred feet deep. If smelt are unavailable, suckers or shiners may do the trick.

Each fisherman is allowed five tip-ups and two hand-lines. Bait, tackle and licenses are available in Schroon Lake, South Schroon, and Pottersville. There are many food establishments open in Schroon Lake for winter fishermen, but motel accommodations are more limited and advance reservations are recommended.

While landlocks and lakers provide much action here, there are many other fish present in Schroon Lake. These include smallmouth and largemouth bass, northern pike, yellow perch, smelt, calico bass, rock bass, sunfish, suckers and various minnows.

Smallmouth bass prefer rocky shelves and shoals. Largemouth bass (not very abundant) prefer weedy portions of shallows. A few good bass spots are as follows: In the north basin, in the bay directly opposite Fowler Avenue on the east shore; around a rock pile just north of the public beach in Schroon Lake village and a good mess of rocks running westerly off the southern tip of the island (this bunch of rocks runs about half way across the lake and then drops off into eighty feet of water); by a big rock shelf off the Narrows Restaurant (this runs from the east shore about half way across the lake); and around the Sunken Island in the south basin. Remember one thing: The shallower areas around these shoals are excellent habitat for the cool water species such as bass, perch, pike and panfish, while the deeper areas are excellent habitat for trout and salmon.

About three miles northeast of Schroon Lake lies Paradox Lake. This lake derives its name from an old Indian word that means "flowing backwards." During the spring, when the thaw is at its peak, the Schroon River (and its Paradox Creek tributary) actually reverses its flow back into Paradox Lake. For a short time, Paradox Lake has no outlet.

Five mile long Paradox Lake has a maximum depth of fifty-two feet. It is divided into two halves, with a narrow, stream-like portion dividing the two sections. The eastern sector has a maximum depth of twenty-seven feet. It is the home of most of the cool water species of fish that reside in Paradox.

To get to Paradox Lake, take Rt. 87 to Exit 28, then go east along Rt. 74 about one mile. It has a public boat launch at the State Campsite located about three miles farther along Rt. 74. There is a fee for parking here. The lake has a surface area of 860 acres. Most of your supplies should be bought before you get there.

Paradox Lake has lake trout, a few landlocked salmon, rainbow trout, smallmouth and largemouth bass, great northern pike, pickerel, lake herring, bullheads, perch, calico bass and numerous other panfish. Rainbow trout and all of the cool water fish are spread throughout the lake. The lake trout here are concentrated primarily in the western sector. Trolling for lake trout is done much the same as it is in Schroon Lake. Most of the productive waters are around the rim of the 52-foot depth level. The inlet to Paradox Lake lies at the easternmost end of the lake. There are mostly weed beds and shallow shelves near here. These make for good winter fishing for perch. Winter perch are one of the finest eating of all fish.

The outlet of Paradox begins at the westernmost end of the lake and flows (except in spring as noted) until it enters the Schroon River just south of Rt. 74. This is a slow flowing stream and has been known to produce some good size brown trout. Of course, you have to get back off the main road, and be there in late spring or early summer.

Paradox Lake has produced lake trout in the 16-20 pound class, rainbow trout up to eight pounds, largemouth bass over six pounds and northern pike over 24 pounds. There are some tackle busters in there yet that will beat these.

The prime lake trout area in Paradox Lake is at the western end of the lake. It resembles a triangle that begins at the western end of the narrows (Brier Point) carrying due west to a point jutting out into the lake from the western end of Grovesnor Bay then due south to a boat house and then easterly back to Brier Point. The maximum depth of this triangle is fifty-two feet with just a few variations. Using the same trolling methods recommended for Schroon Lake, you should troll all around this triangle. Some of the time you should hit it a little higher on the shoulders. This applies summer and winter.

Largemouth bass and northern pike are caught in the weedy sections in the easternmost part of the lake and in the narrows. Fishing through the ice at Smiths Bay (Nueeda Bay) has produced some lunker pike. Pike weighing 22 to 24 pounds have been caught there in each of the past four or five winters.

Perch can be caught in almost every corner of the lake. Fishing for perch in the winter is a favorite pastime for all the local fishermen. Most of it is done on the eastern end of the lake and in Nueeda Bay.

Smallmouth bass can be caught at either end of the lake. Fish for them off the rocky ledges with surface lures cast from a boat just before and after dark. Any of your favorites should work here. You can troll for rainbow trout at either end of the lake. Most of the fishermen use a set of spinners with a trailing nightcrawler. Troll the lure about ten or fifteen feet down.

The portion of the Schroon River that flows into Schroon Lake will be the only part of the river discussed here. It begins at a point just below Exit 30 of the Northway and flows south for about seventeen miles before entering the lake. This seventeen miles would be as the crow flies, though the river actually zigs and zags along its way for probably forty miles or more. Several miles below Exit 30, the river first crosses NY Rt. 9 from east to west. This is known as Deadwater Bridge. This, for all practical purposes, is the beginning of the northern portion of the Schroon River. About a mile south of Deadwater Bridge the river crosses Rt. 9 again, this time from west to east. There is a public campsite at this crossing, Sharp's Bridge Campsite. Between Deadwater Bridge and Sharp's Bridge, Lindsey Brook enters the Schroon River. Almost exactly .5 miles farther south along Rt. 9, there is a small trail that turns right down a slight hill. This is the road that leads to West Mill Brook. It is a wilderness road, traversable by most but not all vehicles. Greenough Road is another access point to the Schroon River. It lies just about two miles below the Sharp's Bridge Campsite.

The section between Sharp's Bridge and Greenough Road winds away from any roads for about two miles. This is one of the best runs on the Schroon River, and it's a good place to spend a day.

Just about a mile south of Greenough Road is Pepper Hollow Road. By taking a right on this road you will first cross West Mill Brook and then you will meet the Schroon River again. The river parallels the road along its full length. The river is now west of Rt. 9 and will not cross again until we get to Schroon River Falls, which is about nine miles farther south. Between Pepper Hollow Road and Schroon Falls, the river parallels U.S. 9 and I-87 all the way and is never very far from either. The section of the Schroon River below Pepper Hollow Road and Black Brook Road (the Port Henry Road) is another section of the river that can be very productive for both brook and brown trout. In between there is one other road crossing, and that is at Frontier Town in the hamlet of North Hudson. This is where The Branch also joins the Schroon River.

This entire section of the Schroon watershed is well stocked with brook trout and brown trout. There are trout in all the tribs as well. The Branch, a tributary flowing east from the Blue Ridge is almost entirely posted by private clubs and permission to fish it is difficult though possible to obtain. Again it should be emphasized that the better fishing would be away from the roads and beaten paths.

The stretch above North Hudson is primarily small stream fishing. Here it is probably best to fish the old fashioned way, i.e. by wading the stream. A flat-bottom boat or a shallow running canoe may be used in some sections, but it will be necessary to get out and portage around many obstacles and sandbars. Speckled trout of around a pound or better have been caught in this section of the Schroon, but be careful in identifying all trout caught. Young salmon are at times very plentiful in this sector. Please be careful in releasing them.

Below North Hudson, the Schroon River becomes a larger river and a lazier one. It meanders its way south and has very little fast water. This is a very good section to fly fish for some sassy brown trout. Fall fly fishing this section has also produced some healthy acrobatic salmon. Even lake trout and pike have been caught this far north during the sucker spawning runs in the spring right after ice-out. This section is best handled by floating a small flat bottom boat or a canoe. There are no major obstacles clear down to the falls at Rt. 9.

Spring fishing for salmon and lake trout is very good in late April and early May in the Schroon River just above where it enters the lake. Trolling a Grey Ghost or other smelt imitation or a small floating Rapala works very well. Once you tangle with a three pound or larger salmon in the river, you will be hooked for life.

About six miles to the west of Schroon Lake and flowing from north to south parallel to Schroon Lake, then turning east to join the Schroon River below the lake, is a beautiful stream of pure mountain waters, Trout Brook. This stream rises in the Hoffman Notch Wilderness area, then flows south toward Olmsteadville. It is well stocked with speckled trout and there is a head of naturally bred trout in the upper reaches and tributaries. If you ever had the desire to taste a meal of freshly caught native brook trout,

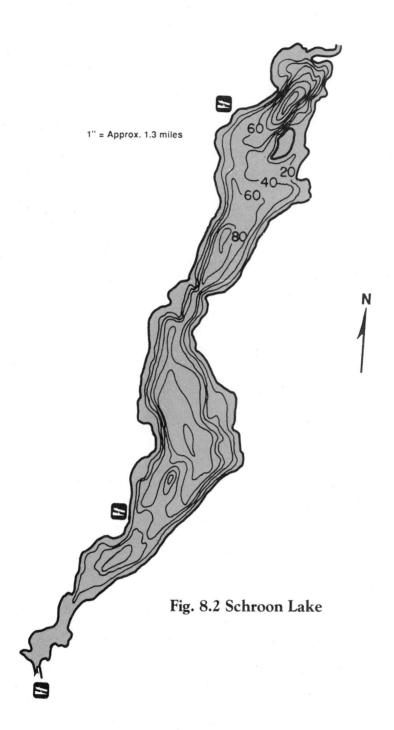

1" = Approx. 1.3 miles

N

Fig. 8.2 Schroon Lake

this is the stream to fish. It is posted in many locations, but permission to cross private lands may sometimes be obtained via a polite request. The best fishing opportunities lie in the upper reaches, where the fish are small but wonderfully good to eat.

To get to this brook, take the Hoffman Road which is located just south of Schroon Lake village on Rt. 9. Go west for about six miles to what is known as Olmsteadville Road. Just prior to hitting this road, you will cross a small stream. This is Trout Brook. Topo maps will show some access spots north of this point. (There aren't any road crossings above here.) Turning south, you will cross the brook in several spots. South of the very next bridge takes you into an area of slow moving water and many beaver dams. This is a good section to fish from a canoe or flat bottom boat.

The waters and wetlands of the Schroon drainage, like all those in the Adirondack Forest Preserve, are of extraordinary value. They support a wide range of wildlife and are also natural recreation areas affording unlimited opportunities for bird watching, wildlife observation, photography, canoeing as well as fishing, hunting and trapping. Please use the utmost care when visiting all these wild areas. Carry out what you carry in, and don't bury anything unless it is readily biodegradable. And always make sure all fires are out before you leave camp.

The Schroon Lake region is one of the most beautiful in New York State. If visitors use it wisely, it can remain so.

Val De Cesare is an avid fisherman and outdoorsman who lives in the Schroon Lake area. He knows the Schroon watershed, and a myriad of surrounding waters, as well as anyone. He is as comfortable on a small brookie stream as he is on a large, frozen-over lake where pike, lake trout and perch are the primary targets.

9

LAKE GEORGE: AMERICA'S MOST BEAUTIFUL LAKE

by Bob Zajac

In the summer of 1642, a gentle Jesuit priest named Father Jogues became the first white man to witness the picturesque beauty and crystal clear waters of Lake George. He had travelled south from Canada via the Richelieu River and Lake Champlain and upon reaching the great body of water, named it Lake of the Holy Sacrament. As a missionary, his purpose was to convert native Americans to Christianity. Unfortunately, the Indians became suspicious of his endeavors as his arrival coincided with a great corn blight. Their convoluted logic resulted in the undermining of the structural integrity of the good Father's skull with a tomahawk. Thus the "Mission of the Martyrs" was sealed with the blood of the lake's discoverer.

Few lakes in our country can rival either the scenic grandeur or the historical significance of Lake George. Its present name is attributed to the Englishman, Sir William Johnson, who in 1754 led his militia north while the colonies were still under the rule of the dull monarch, King George II. In the latter half of the eighteenth century, this region was the violent setting for numerous contests as France and England fought for control of the continent.

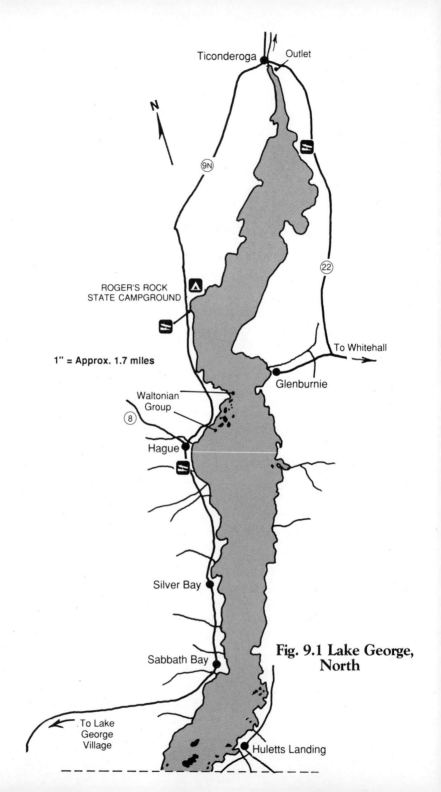

Fig. 9.1 Lake George, North

In literature, James Fenimore Cooper's legendary fictional characters from *The Last of the Mohicans,* Hawkeye, Chingachgook and Uncas, came from Leatherstocking Country to fight near Fort William Henry. Fort Ticonderoga, located at the Narrows, was the keystone of control for one of the most important north-south colonial waterways. During the birth of our nation, many major battles were fought here as the American Revolution crescendoed. Visiting fishermen who are also history buffs should expand their itineraries to include visits to Fort Ticonderoga, Fort William Henry and Crown Point as a minimum.

Lake George, sometimes called America's most beautiful lake, is a product of the late Pleistocene Epoch, also known as the Great Ice Age. It was formed by the scouring retreat of a great glacier that left natural dams on its north and south ends. Runoff from the Adirondacks to the west and the Green Mountains to the east feed its 32 mile length. Rarely more than a mile and a half wide, with a notable maximum depth of 201 feet, the lake offers 28,200 acres of premier fishing. It is easily reached from the Northway (I-87) and Exits 20 through 28 will bring you to the lake with its 365 islands. Yes, one island for each day of the year! You can tour much of the lake's west side by driving Route 9N.

The New York State Department of Environmental Conservation maintains 47 islands for overnight camping by permit only. This allows fishermen to have rods in the water even while the breakfast bacon is frying. An additional eleven islands are maintained for day use only (no permit required) and can provide the scenic setting for a tasty shore lunch. DEC has a separate listing for camping information in the Lake George telephone directory and a quick phone call will provide you with all the necessary details as well as their brochure.

Since Lake George is a vacation resort area, the Warren County Tourism Department (Municipal Center, Lake George, NY 12845) offers a free "Summer Tourist Guide" which lists a multitude of activities, nightlife, attractions, and accommodations for sportsmen and their families. The pamphlet also lists numerous marinas, boat launching and docking sites, bait and tackle shops, guide services, motels, cottages, campgrounds, inns and lodges. The Tourism Department, in addition, provides an excellent free map of the lake showing depth, islands, marinas, restaurants by boat, gas and launch sites.

The Narrows divides Lake George in two, and the halves are known locally as the North Basin and the South Basin, each holding its own secrets. Like Lake Champlain, Lake George is another two-story fishery of impressive dimension. It offers cool water fishing for largemouth bass, smallmouth bass, northern pike, pickerel, and panfish (mainly perch and crappies) as well as good opportunities for its cold water residents, landlocked salmon and lake trout.

Bass season opens the third Saturday in June and closes November 30. For the knowledgeable, fishing is excellent from the opener until early July when the summer temperatures soar. The heat requires a change in tactics as the best fishing will now be found in early morning and again towards evening. The exceptions occur during the rare cool, overcast periods when the fish will feed all day long, especially if the water is choppy. Largemouths show a marked preference for the larger shallow bays which they share with northern pike and pickerel, all taking advantage of the cover in and around weedbeds. The best largemouth habitat will have a gradual drop-off into deeper water adjacent to weed pockets and bottom structure. Plastic worms are a preferred lure, but should be fished painfully slow along the bottom. Night fishing is popular and surface plugs cast close to shore can bring explosive strikes.

Smallmouth bass favor the countless coves, nubs, outcroppings and islands that make the lake famous. These bass, by nature, are schooling fish so if you catch one the odds are there are more in the vicinity. They also show a propensity to school by size, so if you're catching two pounders consistently, you may have to move on to find larger fish. The smallmouths are plentiful and generally any fishy looking structure you encounter will yield fish. For both species, fish deeper toward and through midday, returning to the shallows as the evening sun drops behind the mountains.

In the North Basin, concentrate your efforts for bigmouths on the east shore, specifically in these bays: Mossy, Weed, Heart, Blair and Gull. In the South Basin, you'll find plenty of action in Dunham, Harris, Warner, and Sandy on the east shore, as well as Huddle, Basin, Andrews and Northwest Bays on the west shore.

Favorite smallmouth hotspots in the North Basin are Friend's Point, Stark Point, Gull Bay and Prisoner's Island. In the South Basin, try Diamond Point, Diamond Island, Tea Island, Canoe Island and the islands in The Narrows.

Serious bait fishermen do extremely well with emerald or gold shiners, but bass here also show a marked affinity for crawfish, leeches, frogs and the noble nightcrawler. The well armed lure fisherman will have an arsenal of plastic or rubber worms, six to eight inches long, in black, chartreuse and natural. Spinnerbaits and spoons in the ⅛ to ½ ounce sizes, various crankbaits 1½ to 4 inches long, Luna Tails, Swingblades, and variously colored jigs in sizes from ⅛ to ½ ounce, are also pretty standard fare. Topwater fishermen do well with the old standbys: Hula Poppers, Jitterbugs, Crazy Crawlers, Torpedoes and Crippled Minnows, which are all excellent early in the morning and late in the evening. Actually, any of the chugger, prop or buzz type lures will usually rouse these bass from their haunts. Fly rodders swear by clipped deer hair floaters in a variety of shapes, colors and sizes.

Lake George is one of the true bass hotspots in the east and these fish will honestly average two to four pounds with many fish in the five to seven pound range. The lake is so good that a number of bass tournaments are held here each year, so check the local papers and tackle shops for dates, rules, entry fees and other details.

The season for northern pike and pickerel begins the first Saturday in May and ends about ten months later on March 15. The prime fishing months are May and June with another productive burst of activity from September to freeze-up. In the heat of the summer, pike move to deeper water with structure, and at this time an electronic fish locator is a definite asset.

Hotspots for pike in the North Basin are pretty much the same as for largemouths. In the early morning, try casting in five to ten feet of water along the edges of weedbeds but be aware that these fish will also move deeper as the sun gets higher. Consistently productive areas include Northwest Bay, Dunham Bay, Basin Bay and Harris Bay. In September, when the foliage begins to turn, action seems to pick up near Turtle Island and Mohican Island; however, you may have to go as deep as 35 feet during an Indian Summer. The pickerel are usually found with the northerns and those fishing live bait under a bobber will take their share. Pickerel usually won't take the big eight to twelve inch suckers used for northerns but both of these *Esox* species can and will take anything that they think they can swallow. Top lures for northerns and pickerel are the large Daredevle type spoons in a variety of colors and weighing ⅜ to one ounce. The big Creek Chubs and Rapala type plugs, six to eight inches long, are deadly as are most of the larger crankbaits. Large spinnerbaits are also consistent producers, and pike in particular seem to show a marked preference for an erratic retrieve. Numerous incidental pike catches are made by bass fishermen who fish with bigger lures, especially spinnerbaits. Lake George has a substantial northern population and five to eight pounders are quite common. There are some true monsters in the 20 pound class swimming here so make certain you're using a steel leader when searching for these eating machines.

The panfishing in Lake George is exceptional and a delight for children as well as adults. Panfish can sometimes be caught at will, making these waters an excellent classroom for the small child. There's a crappie run in late April through early May, and 3-pounders will occasionally show up in the Dunham Bay Brook area. There is also an excellent crop of jack perch to be tangled with and many will easily top the two pound mark. Look for them near the sunken island off Hague. Both the crappies and perch provide excellent sport when fished with ultralight gear using small minnows or ⅛ to ¼ ounce spoons or spinners.

Some controversy, not to mention apprehension, has arisen as a result of a new weed problem in Lake George. The source of the issue is Eurasian milfoil, *Myriophyllum spicatum.* This extremely prolific rooted aquatic plant poses a hazard to water skiers and gets a jaundiced look from camp owners and lake users who have had their swimming and docking areas invaded. Primarily a South Basin problem, the first growths of this weed were welcomed by bass and pike fishermen who found great fishing around the new weedbeds. The increase in cover initially enhanced the habitat but this weed unfortunately multiplies at an astounding geomet-

Smallmouth bass is one of the premier gamefish in Lake George. Jumbo small- ies are very plentiful in this clean, rocky lake.

ric rate. Soon the weedbeds became so impenetrably thick that they were all but impossible to fish except around their edges. Any perceived benefit of the plant here was thus short lived. Worse, milfoil's density encourages algae and scum growth which adversely affects water quality and has ruined areas that were once used for spawning. Fortunately, the weed does very poorly at depths of over 20 feet. The Lake George Association recommends hand pulling for removal and has even gone so far as to cover areas of the lake bottom with a black plastic mat in order to block sunlight thereby inhibiting growth. Time will tell what the long range effects of this insidious plant will be, but solutions, if there are any, are not apt to be easy.

Lake George's cold water species are open all year long with size restrictions for lake trout currently at 23 inches and 18 inches or better for landlocked salmon. Current lake limits are three of each species. DEC no longer stocks lake trout here as they reproduce naturally and the population has stabilized at a desired level. However, landlocked salmon continue to be stocked each year and will be until optimal levels are achieved. These fish thrive on smelt and the best fishing coincides with the smelt's spawning run which occurs shortly after ice out (anywhere from late March to mid April) and continues into May. Try trolling, or drift trolling, off shore from smelt spawning streams, about 200 yards out with spoons like the Miller or Sutton Flutters or Lake Clear Wobblers with a trailing worm. Other proven lures are Mooselook Wobblers, Mooneyes in silver, gold or copper, crankbaits like Rapalas and Rebels in smelt colors, and J-Walkers. Early morning and late evening are the most productive hours. Fly rodders will do well trolling Grey, Black or Green Ghosts, Meredith Specials, Supervisors, Nine-Three's, Dark Montreals or any other smelt-like streamer that leaps from the vise screaming to be fished. You might even pick up a rainbow as a bonus. There's a small population that have drifted down from the numerous feeder streams. Interestingly, there is a growing cult of fly fishermen who take salmon in late April by wading out on the Million Dollar Beach in the village of Lake George. The fish are there looking for smelt on their way to spawn in West Brook and it's as good an excuse as any to unlimber your casting arm after a long winter. If you're so inclined to get out and cast some streamers or nymphs in this early season, take the necessary precautions to avoid hypothermia as the water temperature will be well below 50 degrees.

Just after the smelt spawning run ends, the salmon and lake trout will gradually move to slightly deeper water as the warming temperatures force them down to between 35 and 90 feet where

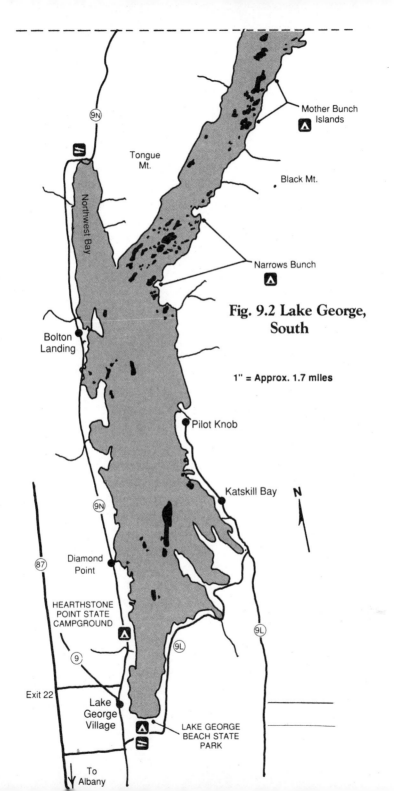

Fig. 9.2 Lake George, South

1" = Approx. 1.7 miles

they are usually found in early June. This is the time for down-riggers or wire or lead core line. In the hottest months of July and August the salmon may be down 50 to 90 feet, but you'll have to go even deeper for the lakers, which will have found comfort between 100 and 180 feet.

In the North Basin, the salmonids concentrate from Hague north to Friend's Point, from Roger's Rock to Indian Kettles, between Blair and Gull Bay, and from Hulett Landing to Mother Bunch Islands off Roger's Rock.

In the South Basin, the lakers and landlocked salmon are found between Diamond Point and Tea Island, between Long Island and Warner's Bay, across the mouth of Dunham Bay, and along the drop-off near Tongue Mountain Point. Summer fishing for salmon and lake trout is a game of odds and an electronic fish locator is now a necessity. Successful anglers know that salmon are comfortable in 50 to 60 degree water but feed in water 55 to 64 degrees. Lake trout seek comfort at 48 to 55 degrees and feed in a strata of 49 to 52 degrees.

In the fall, both species are fairly scattered as the water temperature is cooler and more uniform. Sweep trolling down to 40 feet is the preferred method and offers a welcome return to light tackle as the fish, once again, are found closer to the surface.

The landlocked salmon of Lake George are famous for their sky-rocketing jumps and drag testing runs. An extra rod trolled with the lure in the prop wash, about 15 feet behind the boat, can be an effective trick if the fish aren't taking. These fish will average 2 to 3 pounds, though many between 4 to 6 pounds are taken. Once you hook one, you'll swear they are bigger. The lakers run 8 to 12 pounds but trophy fish of 15 to 18 pounds are landed each year. Anyone fishing Lake George should be aware that the use of smelt as bait (dead or alive) is prohibited. Also, any foul hooked salmon or lake trout must be released.

There are quite a few charter boats on Lake George captained by knowledgeable guides who advertise in local papers, through brochures at tackle shops and as often as not, through word-of-mouth. They are capable of furnishing all equipment and generally operate from inboard/outboards ranging from 20 to 26 feet. Combination packages are offered for both cool and cold water species and you should expect to pay the following rates for a five hour day:

- One person — $110
- Two persons — 135
- Three persons — $160

Guides recommend trolling speeds of about 1½ miles per hour for deep fishing for lake trout and up to 5 miles per hour for land-locks near the surface. Trolling speeds vary with the species, depth and lures. Advanced reservations are a must as these guides are usually quite busy with repeat customers.

If you bring your own boat you should be aware that most bays and passages are zoned with a 5 m.p.h. speed limit and that navigation lights must be used from sunset to sunrise. Also, the following buoy code will be helpful to insure safe travel:

- Black and White Spar Buoy — Marks shallow water. Do not pass between buoy and shore.
- Red Buoy with Red Flashing Light — Standard channel marker rules.
- Green Buoy with Green Flashing Light — Standard channel marker rules.
- White with Quick Flashing White Light — Shallow water nearby.
- Red Pennant — Small craft warning of storm or high winds.

For those seeking winter sport, ice fishing has always been popular on Lake George. The first freeze in the coves usually occurs in late November with safe ice generally found just before the New Year. Tip-ups with minnows are standard for northerns, lakers and salmon, but in late February, those big jack perch seem to come into their own. The game plan now changes to small minnows about two inches long and jigging spoons like the Swedish Pimple. Adding a perch eye always seems to increase the action.

Hotspots for lake trout and landlocked salmon include the

Paulists Fathers area in the South Basin as well as the ice around Dome Island. Huddle Bay also provides its share of tripped flags.

For northerns, try Northwest, Warners or Dunham Bay. Again, remember the importance of a steel leader.

The perch beds seem to change slightly from year to year but Tea and Dome Island remain pretty consistent. Perch fishing through the ice is a social sport on Lake George and finding the perch generally means finding the other ice fishermen which is usually an easy task. Bring your best fishing and hunting stories (the true ones!) and be sure to dress for the cold.

If you're planning an ice fishing trip, the Warren County Information Hotline (518) 793-1300, will provide details regarding daily ice and fishing conditions. Also, there's a DEC Hotline (518) 623-3682, that provides information regarding licenses and regulations.

Robert Zajac is an active outdoorsman who focuses his attention on fly fishing and big game hunting. In the spring, he can be found chasing the hatches throughout New York State. June through August are reserved for Atlantic Salmon, while in autumn he is out pursuing whitetails. He has contributed to several other books and has had articles published in the Atlantic Salmon Journal.

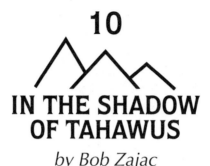

10

IN THE SHADOW
OF TAHAWUS

by Bob Zajac

The civilization of the central Adirondacks began in 1826 with the chance meeting of an ambitious prospecting party and a controversial Abanaki Indian. David Henderson and Archibald MacIntyre hired Lewis Elijah Benedict to lead them to the iron ore deposits that had been the Native Americans' secret. They turned his fee of $1.50 and a tobacco plug into millions when they founded the Adirondack Iron Company a few years later. They called their guide Tahawus, the Indian name for Mt. Marcy or "he splits the clouds." Henderson and MacIntyre left their names on the mountains above Sanford Lake and the settlement near the original forge still bears the name, Tahawus.

The industry spawned towns, and roads linking them have evolved into paved highways. The Tahawus region is accessed by Routes 87, 28, 28N, and 30/8 and consists of portions of Essex, Hamilton and Warren Counties.

Today, lodging, campsites, food, supplies, tackle and bait are available in Indian Lake, Speculator, Wells, North Creek and at most exits along the Northway (87). The DEC office in Warrensburg offers a variety of printed material regarding stocking lists,

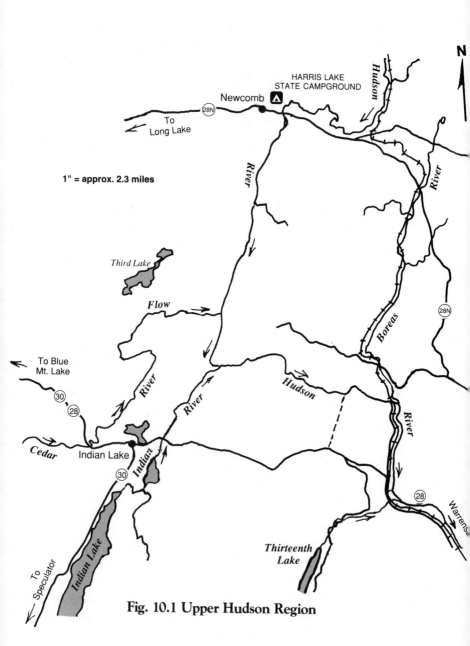

Fig. 10.1 Upper Hudson Region

guide service, maps, etc., and is an extremely important source of information. Fishermen are urged to consult the regulations as they vary considerably by location.

Timing is important as winter is the prodigal son among Adirondack seasons. His tantrums can be felt through April, postponing the early spring enjoyed elsewhere. On many still waters, ice-out doesn't occur until late April and the streams are not sufficiently warmed until May. From May through June is black fly season and an effective repellent is a wise investment in predator control.

Peak fishing for trout and salmon is generally from mid May through mid June. Since these species are extremely temperature sensitive, the best daytime fishing is prior to the heat and low-water conditions of summer. The fishing picks up again considerably in September. The fish seem to feed with urgency during the change of foliage as if they sense the approach of the harsh winter.

The Hudson begins as a trickle from Lake Tear of the Clouds. Its flow increases as it is joined by the Opalescent, Indian and Boreas Rivers. In the spring, it is a powerful river with magnum currents that demand respect when wading. From its junction with the Indian below Blue Ledges downstream to North River, the Hudson offers some of the area's finest fishing for brook, brown and rainbow trout. A popular stretch of water lies adjacent to Route 28 in North River. For those willing to hike, the upper Hudson offers opportunities for a distraction-free escape to a primitive wilderness area. The spectacular Blue Ledges can be reached from the east side of the river by following the North Woods Club Road outside of Minerva to the DEC parking area at the Blue Ledges trailhead. Anglers willing to test their wading skills will be challenged by a variety of riffles, flats, pools and pocket water. Waders with felt soles are recommended to insure the best possible footing. Those who choose not to take this precaution are usually seen doing the Tahawus Shuffle. This sequence of gyrations and spastic gestures bears a marked resemblance to the Indian Rain Dance and generally results in a good soaking.

Enroute to the Blue Ledges the hiker will cross the Boreas

River. This stream should not be overlooked as it offers good rainbow and brook trout fishing. It can be fished upstream or downstream from the crossing point and is a favorite among local anglers, especially near the still water about a mile upstream.

Below North River the Hudson is a series of long shallow flats with the occasional deep pool. As one proceeds south toward the Glen the habitat becomes more conducive to smallmouth bass. They seem to occupy any pool offering reasonable depth.

Glen Creek enters the Hudson from the west and has some very large brown trout that tend to lose their natural caution during a good evening hatch. Although Glen Creek is stocked, the best fishing is near its entry with the Hudson and for a short distance upstream.

The Indian River is a productive trout fishery and can be reached by following Chain of Lakes Road north from Route 28 just east of Indian Lake Village. The fishing begins just below the spillway and offers brook and rainbow trout for several miles to its junction with the Hudson. For those who wish to escape the crowds near the dam, the area above and below the Cedar River junction further downstream is excellent and receives very little pressure. Caution is advised when fishing the Hudson and the Indian as their flow is regulated by the Hudson River/Black River Regulating District. Severe and sometimes sudden fluctuations in water level can occur.

The Sacandaga River and its East Branch are generally accessible as Routes 30 and 8 are rarely far from their banks. The main branch from Speculator to the town of Hope is fair trout water. Augur Falls below Speculator is a photographer's delight. Better fishing is found in the Wells area, just below the Lake Algonquin dam, behind the local lumber yard and in the pools adjacent to the parking areas along Route 30 just south of town. The falls below the dam provides increased oxygen and the series of pools downstream have sufficient depth to sustain brook and brown trout through the summer. As the river flows south toward the Sacandaga Reservoir it becomes more shallow, wider and much warmer, creating habitat for smallmouth bass and panfish. The best of the East Branch is found by hiking north from the Siamese Ponds Trailhead on Route 8 over Eleventh Mountain. In the cool valley below, one can enjoy solitude and native brook trout.

Other streams worth a few casts are the Jessup and Miami Rivers north of Speculator and Mill and North Creeks in the township of Johnsburg, Warren County.

Although not as fertile as the Catskills, the region does have an insect population that generates considerable activity from May through September. Intercepting the hatches is an iffy situation anywhere, so fly fishermen should be prepared to try sub-surface techniques, including streamer fishing and upstream nymphing. The Black Nosed Dace, Mickey Finn and Wooly Bugger streamers (#4-8) and Gold Ribbed Hare's Ear and stonefly nymphs (#8-14) are consistent producers. During July and August, feeding activity is generally confined to early morning and late evening when the water is cool. Exceptions occur during cold, overcast periods when the rivers escape the heat of the sun. It is noteworthy that on occasion, rainbows can be "pounded up" by fishing pocket water with high floating dry flies such as the popular Wulff patterns. These fish seem to prefer the faster currents and can be quite cooperative with this method.

Fly tackle for fishing the streams requires a rod of 7 to 8½ feet for a five or six weight line enabling the angler to present a variety of fly sizes by varying leader length and tippet size. The length of rod is usually a personal choice with the shorter rod favored for smaller streams.

The spin fisherman should be appropriately equipped with light tackle capable of handling six pound test and a variety of spinners and spoons in the ¼ oz. range. The Mepps Spinner, Mepps Minnow, Panther Martin, Phoebe and Little Cleo are all very effective. A favorite bait fishing technique is working a minnow or worm on a #6 hook below a split shot through the riffles and into the depths of the pools.

For those who prefer lake fishing, Indian Lake is highly recommended. Located in Hamilton County, this 4,500 acre impoundment offers beautiful scenery, easy access and a variety of fish. Canoe and boat rentals are readily available and there is a state boat launch. State campsites are located on shore and on several islands as well.

A season on Indian Lake begins in May with northern pike fishing. Techniques include trolling large spoons close to shore and still fishing large minnows or suckers below a bobber in the shallows. The Lake Abanaki area adjacent to Indian Lake near Sabael is popular and produces northerns in the four to ten pound range. There is also a smelt run in May where Squaw Brook enters Indian Lake on the west side.

Beginning in June and continuing through the summer, fishermen are busy casting for smallmouth bass in the two to three pound class. A jig-and-pig, various crankbaits, spinners and spoons are all productive especially on the south and west sides of the lake's many islands. As with many man-made lakes, the bottom is composed of a variety of structure which attracts gamefish. The rock ledges along the east shore are an indication of good water and deserve considerable attention. In the early morning and again later in the evening, top water plugs such as the Hula Popper, Jitterbug and floating Rapala provide exciting bass action, with northern pike adding an occasional explosive surprise.

The best area for landlocked salmon and lake trout is the north end of the lake just above the dam where the water covers the original streambed. Standard trolling techniques will take the occasional fish, but trout fishing has fallen off in recent years due to the severe fluctuations in water level due to releases in the spring and fall.

In addition, Indian Lake has an abundance of perch, bullheads, crappies and other panfish available to the fisherman armed with worms and small children. It is an ideal spot for a family vacation.

There is a special magic associated with brook trout fishing in an Adirondack pond. The horizon is always a distant mountain and the quiet pace can be hypnotic until broken by a rising fish. Thirteenth Lake, Kibby, Peaked Mountain, Puffer and the Siamese Ponds in Warren County are typical of the region. Hamilton County offers Tirrell, Owl and others such as Mason Lake with its added bonus of brown trout.

Spin fishermen generally cast bait, spinners or small spoons while locals, a generation older, cling to the tradition of trolling a worm behind a Lake Clear Wabbler. These techniques are on the decline in recent years due to DEC's efforts to protect these fragile ecosystems. In many ponds, anglers are prohibited from using live bait of any kind as the present population of trout is the product of the countless dollars and hours of effort required to reclaim these fisheries. Shamefully, a number of other ponds have been lost to coarse fish inadvertently dumped from the minnow buckets of violators.

In the late 1870's, Henry Barton began mining garnet in the Gore Mountain area. Ore containing these ruby crystals was abundantly imbedded in the anorthosite crust of nearby mountains as well. The mountains overlooking Thirteenth Lake bear the scars of man's lust for a precious stone. The anglers canoeing Thirteenth Lake bear the passion for other jewels, the brook trout, and landlocked salmon. Recent stockings of Bavarian seeforellen brown trout with their incredible growth rate are an exciting prospect. Hopefully, they will enjoy success.

Thirteenth Lake is a narrow ribbon of water two miles in length resting between Hour Pond Mountain and Balm of Gilead Mountain. It is accessible by car and can be reached via Thirteenth Lake Road which meets Route 28 just west of North River. At the parking area you will note DEC posters defining current special regulations. Legal size and creel limits may vary from year to year, but Thirteenth Lake has been "artificials only" since DEC reclaimed and stocked it in 1972.

Perhaps the most common method of fishing the lake is the slow troll from a canoe or small boat which allows you to peacefully cover the water and enjoy the glorious mountain scenery. A small nymph (#10-14) trailing about sixty feet behind is generally productive throughout the season, but anglers should also be aware of the existence of other opportunities.

In May, the local smelt population begins its annual migration.

Bob Zajac with a fine trout taken in the Tahawus Region. At least a half dozen good trout streams converge in this upper Hudson area.

The aggressive landlocks and larger trout thrive on these fish which were stocked here as forage. The fish seem to congregate where Peaked Mountain Brook enters the lake about one half mile down on the west shore. A smelt streamer can be deadly in this area and at the far (south) end of the lake where beaver have dammed Buck Meadow Flow. The warmer temperatures of spring stimulate insect activity that continues until the summer's heat becomes oppressive. Although trolling may remain a part of the game plan, it is now time to have a second rod ready in anticipation of dry fly activity. Opportunities are numerous when the lake is calm as risers can be seen from a considerable distance, but even the slightest breeze will ruffle the surface making the telltale rings difficult to distinguish even at close range. Midday opportunities occur but at the mercy of the breezes. Shortly after five o'clock, though, the winds seem to settle down for the evening. The trout and salmon now cruise just under the surface in groups, or pods, selectively dining on the insect du jour.

Fish rise to Callibaetis, a size #16 gray mayfly, but the importance of this hatch is generally overshadowed by the presence of caddis that are usually on the water at the same time but in greater numbers. The small moth-like caddis are seen in several life stages: resting on the surface just after hatching, hovering above the water during their mating flights and dipping to the surface depositing their eggs. The most common sizes are #16 and #18 and again the fish seem to be more selective to size than specific dressings.

The Elk Hair, Henryville and skittering caddis patterns are equally effective, but the most difficult aspects of fishing the surface are not fly patterns but approach and presentation. The most efficient method of approach during these "glassed out" surface conditions is to stop paddling a goodly distance away and quietly coast to the fish or get into position and wait until their feeding direction brings them to you. These fish are easily spooked and the complexity of the situation is compounded by the fact that, unlike stream fishing where the quarry maintains a position in a feeding lane, fish in still waters cruise the surface. The constant movement of these fish requires that the angler determine direction, anticipate where the next rise will occur and have his fly waiting there as the fish approaches. Light tippets, long casts, small flies, perfect timing and flawless presentation are the components of success on any Adirondack still water. Taking fish under these conditions provides a great challenge, but even greater rewards.

In May, June and again in September, the hatches can present more challenges or more frustrations as the lake changes its menu. The caddis and mayfly activity continues, but careful observation will yield that the fish may now be stuffing themselves with Diptera. These mosquito-like Chironomids are preferred in their pupal state. Just prior to hatching, the pupa rest suspended in the surface film invisible to the angler who may believe that the fish are rising for no apparent reason. A size #14-#16 imitation of these delicate minutae will produce if the angler maintains his discipline. The degree of difficulty increases dramatically here as the tactics are the same for the caddis and mayfly hatches except you cannot see the fly you are fishing. You strike when there is a rise where you believe your fly to be. This is post doctoral fly fishing and a supreme challenge. It requires perseverance, a bit of masochism and a little Zen.

In early June, brown bodied, grey winged *Hexagenia* mayflies of homeric proportions emerge at the south end of the lake. The hatch usually occurs during the noon to three period allowing the angler to intercept it casually. These insects are a size #8 4XL and demand attention. They will occasionally flutter and fall clumsily back to the water bringing slashing rises from both trout and salmon. This is the hatch that brings the big fish up and a good hex hatch is a spectacle that raises the hair on the back of your neck and leaves memories indelibly etched in your mind.

Although wading is possible, more area can be covered from a canoe. Long casts with nymph imitations stripped back will bring fish but the greatest sport is to be had with the dry fly. It is essential that presentations are gently placed ahead of cruising fish, allowed to rest, and twitched slightly if necessary to induce a rise. Again, these fish have shown selectivity to size more than pattern and large Wulffs, hairwings, and the spider types such as the Grey Fox Variant all have their day.

During the heat of July and August the hatches subside considerably. Although there is generally a hatch just at dark, most fish are taken during the day by deep trolling.

Long rods are an asset for trolling but more important for dry fly fishing from a boat or canoe. The additional length of an 8½ or 9 foot rod allows the seated angler to increase his casting distance by simple laws of physics. Any good single action fly reel with a light, smooth drag will do nicely. Line weight for trolling is not an issue but trying to push a large fly during the hex hatch will require a six or seven weight rod. For the more delicate presentations of smaller flies an 8½ footer for a five or six weight is about right. Leader length for dry fly fishing the ponds should start at about 12 feet.

When playing landlocked salmon or any other leaping fish, it is imperative to "bow" to the fish when he jumps. This means, simply, that when the fish clears the water you should lower your rod tip to put slack in the line to prevent the fish from falling on a taut leader. The landlocks of Thirteenth Lake range from 10 to 21 plus inches, and 16 inches is a lovely fish. They are cousins of the majestic Atlantic salmon, King of Gamefish, and as we bow to them we do so with respect for their genetic heritage.

The brook trout of Thirteenth Lake range from 10 to 18 plus inches and a 14 inch fish would be considered a very good one. The beautiful brookie is the All-American boy that provides us with a link to a great era of Adirondack angling gone by and a symbol of our obligation to preserve these fragile environs for the future.

11

WASHINGTON AND SARATOGA COUNTIES

by Tracy Lamanec

This chapter covers a beautiful region where lush farmfields lap up against the foothills of the Adirondacks and Green Mountains. If I could fish a different place within Washington and Saratoga counties each of my remaining days, I doubt I could sample half of the opportunities the area has to offer.

The northernmost narrow strip of Washington County is bounded on the west by Lake George (Ch. 9) and on the east by the State of Vermont. Here, the southern part of Lake Champlain is so narrow that it is more like a slow moving river than a lake. The New York-Vermont state boundary goes down the center of it. I am most familiar with this part of Champlain for ice fishing, and we'll begin the discussion there.

The usual catch includes lots of small yellow perch, occasional northerns close to shore, walleye in the dredged shipping lane, a few small saugers and once in a while a real bragging size walleye. Golden shiners and spot-tailed shiners, available in bait shops in Whitehall and elsewhere, are the usual bait. Between hungry perch and wind flags, one often doesn't have time to get out the 15 tip-ups allowed on this lake. But if things get slow, I jig with a gold Rapala or Swedish Pimple and perch eye. Sometimes the jig will keep me so busy I don't need the tip-ups.

Whole villages of ice shanties spring up and the fishing derbies that are held throughout the winter create a carnival atmosphere. South Bay is a lake in itself. Many of the smaller bays are shallow and weedy. They see much less fishing pressure and can produce buckets of small yellow perch. If that sort of thing excites you, try Mill Bay at Putnam Station or Pine Lake Brook Bay. Red Rock Bay and all locations on the Vermont side require a Vermont fishing license.

There can be some outstanding early season stream trout fishing (minnows are recommended) in the Poultney River which forms the boundary with the Green Mountain State. Another excellent bet for the early season trout fisherman is the Mettawee River, which enters New York State at Granville. It has slow, deep pools, some unfortunately littered with old auto parts and appliances. Other sections of this stream, plus the Indian River which crosses Rt. 22 just south of town, have stretches of fast water that are strewn with the spoils of slate quarries. Appearances can be deceiving. Those pools and riffles harbor big rainbows. Salted minnows are most effective in the early season.

Halfway Creek is a small but respectable trout stream that is mostly accessible from Rt. 149 in the town of Fort Ann. In evidence are some gravel bottomed riffles, but look for the larger trout in deep pools where this meandering pasture stream undercuts its banks.

The fabled gem of the area for the fly fisher is the Battenkill. It is truly a blue ribbon trout stream. Moderate fertility, reasonably dependable fly hatches, and a combination of width, depth, and gradient that make it easy to wade and fly cast over have contributed to its popularity. The pastoral setting and the knowledge of its rich significance in the history and literature of fly fishing can make a few hours on the Battenkill a most relaxing and soul cleansing experience. A sparse human population and a tenacious guardianship of the river by influential people and organizations (for example the Clearwater Chapter of Trout Unlimited) have combined to maintain the river's high quality. As rural Vermont and nearby New York continue the transition from a cheese and maple syrup economy to upscale second homes and real estate speculation, the defenders' strength of will will be tested.

From where the stream enters New York to the covered bridge at Eagleville, just over four miles, special regulations apply. This stretch is all easily accessible from state Rt. 313. Less traveled Hickory Hill Road, Camden Valley Road, Robinson Road, and Eagleville Road follow the opposite side of the river. There are formal angler access paths and parking areas provided by the state, but the state's easement applies only to the stream bank. Much of the access is over private land. It is easy to spot the pull-offs where generations of other fishermen have parked near bridges or just pulled off to the side on Rt. 313, County Rt. 61, and Eagleville Road. For the most part, the landowners have resigned themselves to the situation and only ask for your respect. You will see angler access signs, and other signs detailing the special regulations in effect on the stream. Others just say "NO BAIT." But signs have a way of coming down, so consult the special regulations, by county, in New York State's Fishing Regulations Guide.

Having fished the river for several years before the special regulations, I will offer some observations as to their effects. First, they have tended to concentrate the fishermen on the special water. Consequently, it has lightened the pressure on the river downstream of this. As for the size limits, I feel they are counterproductive. They seem to cause the population to become dominated by smaller fish by cropping off most trout once they get within $\frac{1}{8}$ inch of the legal size. A more insidious long range effect is that selectively removing most of the large, predatory trout allows the small trout and non-game fish to become overpopulated. Chubs, shiners, dace, and suckers compete more successfully with small trout. Eventually only trout that mature sexually before reaching the legal size live to reproduce. This selective breeding may be producing a race of trout of smaller size and shorter life expectancy.

When first instituted, the special regulations included a 12-inch size limit. It has since had to be reduced to ten inches. Will it be eight inches in a few years?

Some of these inferior trout undoubtedly move downstream, but if you choose to fish below the special regulations section you will find some differences. First, you will meet far fewer fishermen. When I want to meet fishermen I go to a TU meeting or hang out at a tackle shop. Secondly, you will probably catch fewer trout. What you will notice is that the trout you do catch will cover a more natural distribution of sizes. Few will have hook scars and missing mouth parts. Your chances of connecting with a few that will put a bend in your rod and strip line from your reel will be greatly improved.

I highly recommend the stretch below Shushan. It is accessible only by wading or by walking along the railroad bed, either downstream from town or up from Rexleigh. It is the most secluded stretch of the river. More accessible but still offering comparative solitude is the stretch upstream from Shushan, along county Rt. 64. There is a good stretch accessible by walking downstream from Eagleville Bridge to Rt. 64.

The Battenkill between the bridges at East Greenwich and Battenville may be accessed from state Rt. 29 on one side or Skellie Rd. on the other. But these roads only meet the stream at a couple of points. Points in between require crossing farmers' fields and permission should be sought. The hospitality with which you are greeted will depend on the impression left by the previous fisherman. I like this section especially where the river divides around a series of islands.

The entire river is easily drifted with a canoe, providing the angler access to the most remote pools. Expect to get out and drag over gravel bars when the water gets low. Non-angling canoeists in numbers to make fishing difficult are sometimes encountered. Weekends in May on the upper stretches are the worst. On hot summer afternoons, swimmers in inner tubes present similar problems.

For years I made after-work and weekend excursions to the Bat-

tenkill at least once a week throughout the season. The highlight of the insect activity comes early in the form of the hendrickson hatch, which starts as early as mid April and lasts into mid May. The peak is about May 1 and it tends to progress up the stream. Some years, high water makes it almost impossible to fish. At the peak, trout are nymphing by noon and still taking duns at five. As the hatch progresses, it gets later in the day and becomes of shorter duration.

The hendrickson hatch is followed by caddis hatches that can often frustrate the angler's attempts at correct imitation. In the way of subsurface imitations, the Hare's Ear and Breadcrust can be productive. On top, I have had considerable success during heavy caddis activity by skittering a bivisible over the riffles. I tie it with furnace hackle over most of the hook and a collar of grizzly. Use larger hackle than appropriate for the hook size, typically a #14. Trim it with sharp scissors to look like a bottle brush. With some floatant, it will pop up like a cork if dragged under. The same fly is good for prospecting in white water pockets on the Ausable or as a strike-indicating dropper when fishing a nymph.

Leisurely fishing to slow paced evening hatches of light cahills and other light-colored flies can be enjoyed throughout the summer. One of my favorites is the *Potamanthus,* a large buttery-yellow mayfly that comes off just at dark. Various blue-winged olive hatches also occur on this river in summer.

I learned to fish a gang of large wet flies after dark while grow-ing up in the Catskills. It is very effective on the Battenkill when the heat of summer causes trout to sulk in the shade all day. In sev-eral years of collecting scale samples, I found trout caught at night to average one year older than those caught during the day. Trout grow a few inches in a year.

Forget just briefly what you have learned from fishing small dry flies. For night fishing, I use a level monofilament leader that is 20 to 25 pound test minimum and is no longer than my rod. Put a loop at the end, middle, and halfway between to accommo-date three flies in a range of sizes from six down to two tied on snells of the same leader six to ten inches long. The heavy lead-er, because of its stiffness, keeps the whole mess from getting tangled as easily and makes the flies work relative to one anoth-er. It has the advantage of being able to break off dead limbs and uproot small trees that you may hang up on in the dark.

My favorite patterns are the Professor, all the variations on the Coachman, and most of all, the Red Tipped Governor. Let the rig swing across the current in moving water. In still water, use a slow hand-twist retrieve and be prepared for explosive strikes.

It helps to be very familiar with the hole you are fishing. The darker the night the better. Above all, don't shine a light on the water. I have caught several bats, a muskrat that put up a vicious fight and a raccoon that broke me off.

Summer mornings on the Battenkill require the other extreme. Various midges and tiny mayflies either emerge or return to the water as spinners most of the second half of the season. Long, fine tippets and #24 spent-winged flies are in order.

Midday in hot weather is best dealt with by napping in the shade. If you insist on fishing, wear a broad brimmed hat with polaroid glasses. Much of the stream lends itself to wading the center and casting to the banks. You will spot trout finning in the shade of overhanging bushes. A stealthy approach followed by a brief rest before casting a black ant just upstream of your intend-ed target will bring results. Another good pattern for these conditions

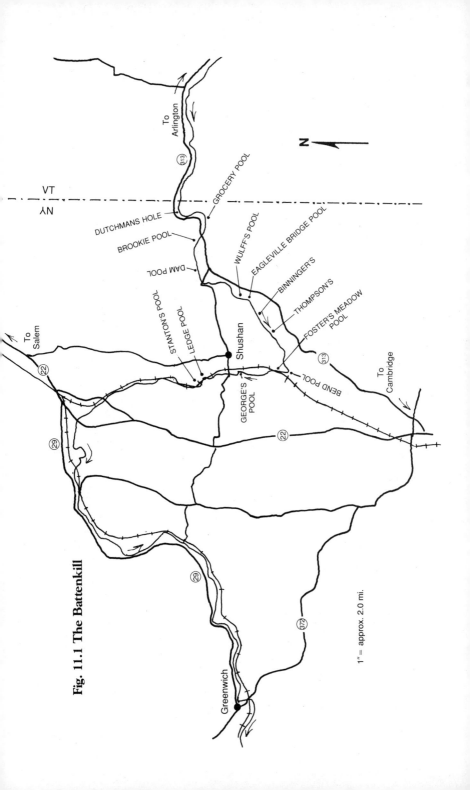

Fig. 11.1 The Battenkill

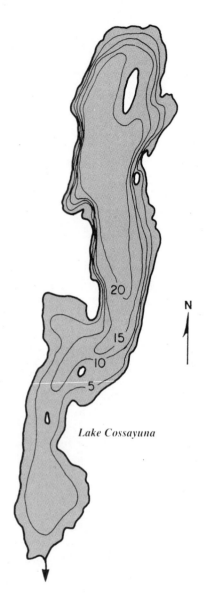

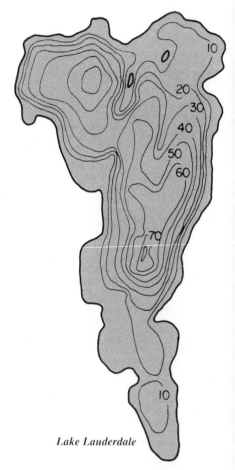

1" = Approx. .12 miles

N

Lake Cossayuna

Lake Lauderdale

Fig. 11.2 Lakes Cossayuna & Lauderdale

is the indispensable Muddler Minnow, but loaded with floatant and twitched on the surface to imitate a grasshopper.

Several small tributaries enter the Battenkill and most hold fish. They tend to be ignored for good reasons. First they are on private land. Second, they are so small that they offer little space for fly-casting. Their significance to the Battenkill fly fisherman should not be overlooked, however. Where they enter the main stream they often produce conditions that cause trout to congregate. In hot weather, much of the flow in these little valleys is underground. These "seeps" enter the river near the mouths of these streams. Conversely, in early spring, the ground water carried by these valleys may be warmer than the main river. This, too, can attract trout. Further, runoff from a summer thundershower will bring a lot of food down the tributaries. They are also important to the natural reproduction that sustains the population of wild trout. Best known of these are Camden Creek, Murray Hollow Brook, Steele Brook, Juniper Swamp Brook, and Black Creek. A bait fisherman who takes the time to talk to landowners and do some exploring could be well rewarded.

Moving on, the Hoosic River forms part of the southern boundary with Rensselaer County between Eagle Bridge and Buskirk. It deserves mention in any discussion of fishing in Washington County, but it does not rival the Battenkill as a trout stream, and is mostly in Rensselaer. White Creek is a significant tributary. What was said about the tributaries of the Battenkill also applies to those of the Hoosic.

Other than Lakes George and Champlain at the north end of Washington County, covered fully in other chapters, there is a string of small lakes down the county's center. These include Cossayuna, Hedges, Schoolhouse, and Lake Lauderdale. They are all surrounded by private land and camps, which puts a limitation on access. They are predominantly cool water fisheries. Though none of these has a big reputation, people I have talked to who fish them always have good stories to tell.

The smallest of the lakes is Dead Pond. It is very accessible, right

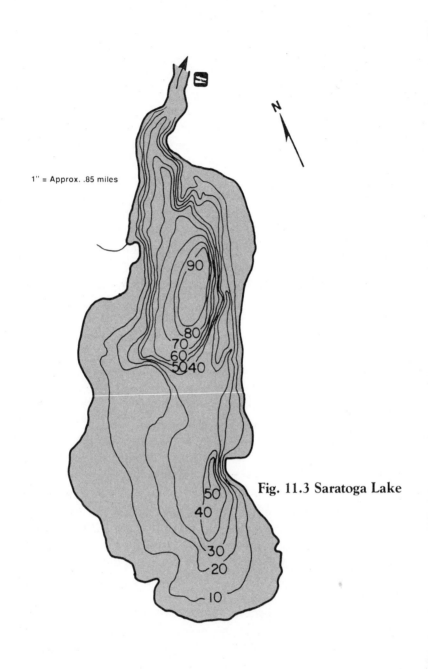

1" = Approx. .85 miles

N

90

80
70
60
5040

50
40

30
20

10

Fig. 11.3 Saratoga Lake

at the intersection of state Rt. 22 and county Rt. 61. The pond has been reclaimed and is heavily stocked with trout. Each year's stocking includes a few big old hatchery breeders. Families of anglers with rods propped up on forked sticks and Coleman lanterns are the usual sight as I drive by on my way home from fishing an evening hatch on the Battenkill.

Saratoga County also has a lot of cool water species opportunities. Many of the small ponds abound with pickerel, perch, and bullheads, while some of the bigger waters have reputations for northern pike, walleye, and bass. Best known of these is Great Sacandaga Lake, which is covered in another chapter.

One cool water lake that is good — although small and ringed by private camps and homes — is Galway. Some of the best fishing is along an old causeway that is above the surface in summer when the lake level is drawn down. Every property owner on the lake I spoke with assured me that the very best fishing was right from his own dock. Galway has one of the best largemouth populations in the area.

Saratoga Lake, Round Lake, and Ballston Lake are all outstanding cool water fisheries. They are very fertile, so summer brings excessive weed growth and algae blooms. I am most familiar with Saratoga, the largest of the three. It is a favorite of ice fishermen, including this one. With a good hand auger, a plastic bucket, a jig stick and a Rapala, you're all set. Head out from Mangino's Restaurant at the south end, or Brown's Beach area on the southeast side of the lake toward the middle of the south basin, and catch some of the largest and most colorful yellow perch found anywhere. They travel in schools so it takes some exploring, but somewhere south of Snake Hill in 25 to 35 feet of water you should find them. They will usually be near the bottom at first, but will often follow a hooked fish right to the top.

Shallower, weedier water along the east side either south or north of Snake Hill and over on the west side near the inlet at Chinatown are the places to find northern pike that are bigger than in most other area waters. The best walleyes come from the

Big bass are another strong possibility in these counties just outside the Capital District. Saratoga Lake is a top bet.

deeper water near the middle of the south basin. Though jigging for perch often produces a walleye or northern, they are best taken via the waiting game of tip-ups and shiners. Don't be afraid of using too big a bait. This is a case where the old adage, "big fish, big bait" seems to be affirmed. I have had the best walleye fishing at night. A friend and I rigged our tip-ups with penlight bulbs and AA batteries so that when the flag comes up, the spring makes electrical contact to signal a fish in the dark.

When spring comes, fishing activity centers around the walleye and northern pike spawning runs at the inlet. The opening of the season is controlled to give spawners some protection. As the water warms, smallmouth and largemouth bass upstage the other species. Plastic worms do best before the weeds become fully developed, while weedless spinnerbaits fished along the edges of the weed beds work better later, and they also catch some northerns. Large surface plugs (or fly rod popping bugs) cast from a canoe to the weed edges at dusk or dawn can provide some of the most enjoyable action to be had on Saratoga lake.

Much of Saratoga County is bounded by river. The Mohawk on the south is a popular and very productive smallmouth fishery. It is also stocked with tiger muskies, providing a chance at a real lunker. *Good Fishing In The Catskills,* in this same series of books, covers the Mohawk in detail.

Many of Saratoga County's lakes and rivers hold enormous carp. They may be taken quite reliably on gobs of Wheaties. That's right, *"The Breakfast of Champions"!* Hold a handful under water until soggy, then compact them into a ball on a small treble hook. Carp are a highly prized game and table fish throughout Europe and most of the world. American anglers look down their noses at them and seem to be content to leave carp for the bow fishing contests. Carp fishing is an excellent way to introduce a young angler to the awesome power of a large fish that won't break your heart if it gets away.

The best known trout stream in Saratoga County is the Kayaderosseras. It has some good fly hatches but is considerably smaller than the Battenkill and not as easy to fish. Most of its tributaries hold sizable brown trout but few fly fishermen are willing to try to cast in the confined quarters of overhanging brush. A fat nightcrawler tumbled along the bottom following a summer thundershower is the best way to put one of those beauties in your creel, if you have one big enough.

In both counties, there are abundant small streams and some ponds teeming with colorful and cooperative little brookies. Most require some walking. The anticipation of what's around the next bend and the sense of exploration can more than make up for the modest size of these fish.

The Hudson river forms the boundary between the two counties. From Hudson Falls downstream to the Troy Dam all fishing is banned. The reason given by the state is that the river bottom and its fish are contaminated with toxic chemicals. However, there is very good fishing to be found in the Hudson upstream of the prohibited area, and it is largely overlooked. For further information on fishing waters in these two counties, contact the DEC office in Warrensburg. They have lots of up-to-date data such as stocking lists and contour maps of some lakes. Be sure to check the special regulations by county, and the special section on Lake Champlain in your NYS Fishing syllabus. Finally, specific to the Battenkill, I recommend *An Angler's Guide to the Battenkill in New York State* published by the Clearwater Chapter of Trout Unlimited. Incorporating a detailed stream map, it also gives information on hatches, fly patterns and techniques, all contributed by local TU members who fish the river religiously.

Tracy Lamanec grew up on a trout stream in Greene County's Catskill Mountains. He has had a keen interest in shooting, fishing, nature and conservation since childhood. While working for GE in Schenectady, he wrote a weekly outdoor column for 13 years for the Schenectady Gazette. *He has held office in the New York State Outdoor Writer's Association, the New York State Conservation Council, Trout Unlimited and several sportsmen's clubs. He currently resides near Pattersonville with his wife Eileen.*

12

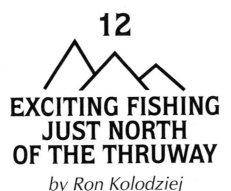

EXCITING FISHING
JUST NORTH
OF THE THRUWAY

by Ron Kolodziej

Wayfaring anglers using the New York State Thruway as a jump-ing-off point will find top-notch opportunities not only within the Adirondack Park Blue Line, but in the fringe areas as well. Let's now consider one such area.

Spread out your map of New York State and locate Amsterdam, just west of Albany. Now draw a line due north to the commu-nity of Edinburg on the shores of Great Sacandaga Lake. From there extend your line due west to Alder Creek and then due south along Route 12 to Utica. Now trace a line over the Thruway back to where you started. If you fish anywhere within this rough-ly rectangular area you're never much more than 35 to 40 miles from the Thruway, as the crow flies, but you have access to some 1,500 square miles of superb fishing opportunities, ranging from record-breaking northerns to bragging-size native brook trout.

Let's begin our odyssey at Great Sacandaga Lake on the east-ern edge of our inscribed area. Created in 1930 as a flood control impoundment by construction of a large earthen dam at Con-klingville on the Sacandaga River, this lake produced a world record northern pike in 1940. It was a magnificent 51½ inch, 46 pound 2 ounce fish that held the world record for almost 40 years. Although it was eventually bested by a European fish, it still lays claim to the North American record for that species.

The halcyon days for Sacandaga Reservoir, as it was then called, lasted through the mid-50's. By that time the richly fertile farmlands inundated by the impoundment had leached the last of their nutrients into the water. Fluctuating water levels and a general lack of forage fish caused a gradual but perceptible decline in the fishery, but it eventually stabilized and still offers great year-round fishing for northerns, walleyes, yellow perch and bass in season. Conventional fishing methods for these species will work well on Great Sacandaga. Drift fishing with Lake Clear Wabblers and a trailer hook baited with a nightcrawler or minnow is a good, productive technique for walleyes and perch. Cabela's Walleye Wobble Jigs in fluorescent red and green are proving to be excellent on the lake's walleyes. Drift fished live bait can also prove deadly on that species. Sacandaga's smallmouths respond well to crawfish, hellgramites and minnows but also to a variety of artificials such as Mepps spinners and various crankbaits. The average Great Sacandaga walleye will weigh in the one to two pound range with six to seven pounders being taken annually. Smallmouths will also average one to two pounds with occasional five pounders.

For the past dozen or so years, good sized brown trout have become a welcome though infrequent bonus at Sacandaga for many anglers, including ice fishermen. Browns up to five pounds have been reported and though not present in great quantities they do crop up often enough to have become less of a topic at local watering holes. These browns are products of stocking programs in area streams feeding the lake and most are taken on live bait though some fall prey to trolled spoons and spinners.

Over the past several years a number of big, 8 to 12 pound catfish have also been taken in the lake though the reader is cautioned against visiting Great Sacandaga specifically for that species. They're uncommon at best, and it's not known what their population level is or how they came to be in the lake. Escape from area farm ponds seems to be one plausible explanation.

If Sacandaga's big northerns are your quarry, plan on shore fishing with big minnows. Few really big fish are taken by other methods such as casting or trolling. Trophy-hunting pike aficionados stake out a piece of accessible shoreline, generally in the lake's shallower southwest basin between the communities of Mayfield and Broadalbin, and rig up light salt water or heavy duty freshwater gear baited with 12 to 15 inch suckers. Then it's a waiting game. Prime time is May and early June when water levels are high and the northerns are still in the shallower, flooded portions of the shoreline before, during and after spawning. If trolling is your preferred method, use large Daredevles in traditional red and white, or jointed Rapalas, Rebels or similar lures in perch or other natural finishes. Depending upon time of day, weather and water conditions, and depth, your best trolling speeds will be between 1½ and 2½ mph. For the most part, you'll be trolling water less than ten feet deep.

Boat launches are available at Northville on the Sacandaga River, at the Northampton Beach Campsite just south of Northville, in the town of Day in the northeast arm, and near the village of Broadalbin. These are state-operated, free facilities but commercial launches can also be found liberally scattered around the lake. However, shorebound anglers on Great Sacandaga need not feel left out. Access to good shore fishing areas is readily available along much of the lake's 125 mile shoreline. I recommend the areas around Northville and Batchellerville Bridges, along much of the Sacandaga River paralleled by Route 30, and numerous roadside areas in the lake's northeast arm.

Many of the streams draining into Great Sacandaga hold fine populations of brook, brown and rainbow trout. You might consider Hans, Kenyetto and Sand Creeks. These and other streams, including the Sacandaga River, are generously stocked with trout by the New York State Department of Environmental Conservation and are generally lightly fished for most of the season. Because of the nature

Twenty pounds of Great Sacandaga northern. Fish twice this size may yet lurk in the lake where Peter Dubuc once took a world record pike.

of the terrain in the Great Sacandaga area, streams can range from slow moving, sand bottomed watercourses to typical boulder-strewn mountain streams with numerous pools and riffles. Any bait or tackle shop, service station or general store can direct you to the nearest trout stream and can suggest the best way to fish it. Information available from the NYS Department of Environmental Conservation and the Fulton County Chamber of Commerce will also help you pick out the streams you may want to fish.

We'll depart Great Sacandaga now and head west on Route 30A and 29A in search of other piscatorial adventures. A half-hour drive from Great Sacandaga brings us to Peck Lake on Route 29A. This is an eminently fishable, privately owned body of water that holds excellent populations of northerns, largemouths, smallmouths, pickerel and an abundance of panfish, and has consistently produced prize-winning fish. The most recent was the second place largemouth bass in the June, 1989 edition of the big, statewide Genesee New York State fishing contest. It tipped the scales at 7 pounds 4 ounces. This 1,400-acre lake has a maximum depth of about 40 feet and features the type of rocky, stump-filled structure that seems to spell fish. Launch facilities, camping, cottages, bait, and boat and motor rentals are available at the lake. Rates and additional information can be obtained by writing to the address at the end of this chapter.

A few miles north, near the intersection of Routes 10 and 29A, we encounter East and West Caroga Lakes, both top-notch fishing waters. They offer a mixed bag of everything from bass to splake to panfish. Walleyes have recently been stocked here and offer additional sport. The lakes are also popular ice-fishing destinations. The shorelines are pretty well filled by summer homes and camps but fishing access is still available. There's a popular

Pretty Peck Lake is as fishy as it looks. See the text for the pleasant options available here.

state-operated campsite on East Caroga, off Route 29A, and launch facilities are also offered. Boat passage between the two lakes is made easy by a small connecting channel.

A stone's throw away, on route 10/29A, is Canada Lake. The 525 acre lake has a maximum depth of about 144 feet and holds lake trout which are stocked annually by DEC. Pickerel, small-mouths and panfish are also present in generous numbers. There are commercial boat liveries on the lake as well as a state-operated launch site. Pine Lake, a few miles north of Canada Lake, also offers good pickerel, bass and panfish angling.

Let's now do some walk-in fishing. Nine Corner Lake lies just west of Pine Lake and is easily reached by a gentle trail less than a mile long. The well-marked trailhead is located on Route 29A, a few hundred feet beyond where 29A and 10 part company. Nine Corner has suffered a bit from acid rain but liming has helped and it receives generous annual infusions of brook trout. Shore fishing access on this body of water is excellent though a canoe or inflatable will help you cover more of the bays that give it its name. If conditions are right you may even get a look at the resident loons. Fish this water as you would any north country pond, but I again recommend a Lake Clear Wabbler with a worm-baited trailer hook. It works as well on trout as it does on Great Sacandaga's walleyes. If fishing from shore, try small Mepps spinners, Phoebes and similar lures.

We are now traveling west on Route 29A. Various trailheads along the way lead the angler to other, more remote fishing waters. If stream fishing is your preference you may want to consider any of a dozen or more streams that course through this area and harbor scrappy browns, brookies or rainbows. Those that are stocked annually by DEC include Caroga, McQueen, May-field and Zimmerman Creeks, to name just a few. A good topo or county map will help you locate these creeks as well as others that are not stocked but hold native populations of trout. DEC also publishes annual stocking reports which will help you track down waters you may want to fish.

The next port of call in our westward trek along Route 29A and then 29 is East Canada Creek. Flowing south out of the Ferris Wild Forest, East Canada offers fine fishing for brookies and browns. It's a clear, cold water stream that features deep holes, tempting riffles and stretches that beckon to the fly fisherman. East Canada is good fishing water throughout the trout season, even during the warmer months. As we traverse Route 29A and then hook up with 29, bear in mind that the area to the north is as wildly beautiful and remote as areas found deeper in the Adirondacks. Fishing opportunities abound and are much too numerous to mention here but this is where homework is important. Again, a good topo map, some imagination and all the information you can gather will open up dozens of new and exciting fishing opportunities for you.

At Middleville, Route 29 hooks up with Route 28. Follow this road up to Route 365 and you're in the extreme northwest corner of our area. Here you'll find Hinckley Reservoir. With some 24 miles of shoreline, a picnic area, boat launch and a recreation area it offers an excellent northcountry angling and camping opportunity. Hinckley is another of those mixed bag waters with something for everyone — pickerel, some trout, bass, panfish and more.

Let's backtrack now. That beautiful, tempting stream you were crossing and paralleling as you traveled northward on Route 28 was West Canada Creek, once rated in the top five of New York State's top 50 trout streams. To our Native Americans it was "Canata" — stream of amber water. Primarily brown trout water, West Canada is popular and productive throughout the season, attracting trout fans of every ilk — waders, bank walkers and canoeists. It supports a healthy native population of trout, generously complemented by some 30,000 hatchery-bred brethren stocked annually along its length. During the summer months it produces some good sized bass in certain areas but big trout are what you're here for. West Canada features big, deep, slow-moving stretches as well as faster water, offering every angler the opportunity to pursue his or her favorite method of angling. For most, however, this is prime fly fishing water and all I can suggest by way of patterns is to "match the hatch." Mayfly, nymph, black gnat, Coachman — you name it, it will produce as on any other trout water at the appropriate time and place. Your favorite spinner or small crankbait will also work well. Bait fishermen will find that live minnows or worms drifted near the bottom will consistently produce trout.

In the early spring, West Canada runs high and fast and this will dictate your fishing methods more than any other factor. The area below the dam at Trenton Falls is subject to sudden water releases from the power generating plant located there. There are no set schedules for these releases and the wading angler should be constantly on the alert for signs of rapidly rising water. This is especially important in the Trophy Section below the falls, which begins at Trenton Falls Bridge and extends about 2.5 miles downstream to the mouth of Cincinnati Creek. The creel limit is three, minimum size 12 inches, and artificial lures only are allowed. Route 28 parallels West Canada for much of its length and roadside access is readily available for miles of excellent trout fishing.

Continuing south on Route 28 you can hook up with Route 29 at Middleville and head east through the southern reaches of our designated area. You're probably tired of fishing by now but there's plenty left as we head back along Route 29 to Route 30 and our starting point. As you're heading back east along Route 29, plan on fishing Spruce Creek in the township of Salisbury. It's great water and harbors some fine brown trout. Spruce enters the East Canada at Dolgeville and you'll be paralleling the creek for a while before entering the village. Other trout waters on your route back include Middle Sprite and Meco Creeks.

We've completed our cook's tour through waters inhabited by bass, northerns, trout, walleyes, bullhead, splake, pickerel and every imaginable species of native New York State panfish — all a stone's throw from wilderness to the north and the Mohawk Valley immediately to our south. Staying on the roads plotted in

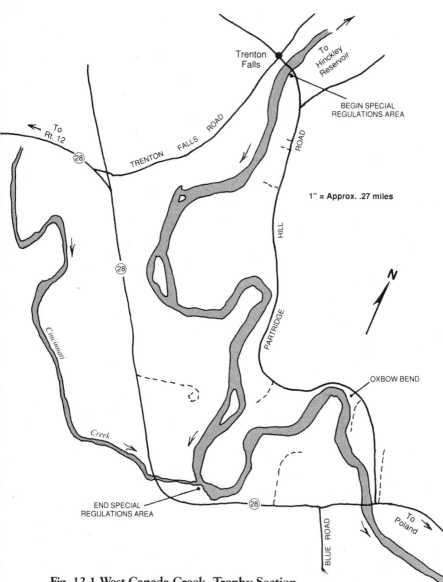

Fig. 12.1 West Canada Creek, Trophy Section

this chapter will keep you within 25 miles of the New York State Thruway most of the time, but the angling opportunities you'll encounter are more than you could handle and do justice to in a dozen seasons.

WHERE TO WRITE FOR MORE INFORMATION

Great Sacandaga Lake Association
Box 900
Northville, NY 12134

Fulton County Chamber of Commerce
18 Cayadutta Street
Gloversville, NY 12078

Great Sacandaga Lake Chamber of Commerce
PO Box 911
Northville, NY 12134

Great Sacandaga Lake Fisheries Federation
Box 991
Northville, NY 12134

Peck Lake Fishing Resort
Route 29A
Gloversville, NY 12078

Ron Kolodziej is an ardent fisherman and hunter who lives in Amsterdam, New York, and has fished extensively "just north of the Thruway." An outdoor columnist for the Amsterdam Recorder *for more than 16 years, he has also written for* New York Game & Fish, Upland Fishing *and southern Adirondack area newspapers. He is an active member of many outdoor groups, including the New York State Outdoor Writer's Association, Whitetails Unlimited, and the Great Sacandaga Lake Fisheries Federation.*

13

THE GREAT SOUTHWESTERN WILDERNESS

by Don Williams

What is the remotest area in northern New York? It's a common muse of both backpackers and anglers. Certainly, the Cold River area west of Mt. Marcy is very remote. So is the interior portion of Tug Hill. And the upper Oswegatchie is very far from anything.

But perhaps the largest wild area of the Adirondacks is what we will call the Great Southwestern Wilderness.

Nine topographical quadrangles define this region: Raquette Lake, Big Moose, Number Four, McKeever, Old Forge, West Canada Lakes, Piseco Lake, Ohio and Remsen. This vast area encompasses some 1.3 million acres, much of it public or "state" land. Route 28 runs through the upper portion of this area while Route 8 slices through the lower part. Both highways intersect with Route 30 (the Adirondack Trail) on the east, and Route 12 on the west.

The Southwestern Adirondacks abound with state land, some of it designated Wilderness and some Wild Forest. Unit Management Plans have been developed by the Adirondack Park Agency and DEC, and these define the usage of this part of the Adirondack Forest Preserve. The Ha-De-Ron-Dah Wilderness Area, West Canada Lake Wilderness, Moose River Plains Wild Forest, and Black

River Wild Forest, along with portions of Pigeon Lake Wilderness and Ferris Lake Wild Forest are all found within the Great Southwestern Tract. In this unspoiled setting you can hunt, hike, ski, canoe and fish. In the wilderness areas, there will be neither sounds nor sights of civilization. In the wild forest areas some motorized use may be permitted. Old wood roads and trails open up the remote fishing ponds and streams to the avid angler. State campgrounds include Alger Island, Brown Tract Pond, Fourth and Eighth Lakes, Golden Beach, Limekiln Lake, Hinckley Reservoir, Nicks Lake, Little Sand Point, Point Comfort, and Poplar Beach.

This region has spawned fish stories for a long time. In fact, stories of great catches have been circulating since the 1840 Lake Piseco Trout Club reports in the American edition of Izaac Walton's *Compleat Angler.* Those who read the book remember the two tons of trout taken from Piseco Lake in a five year period

Piseco Lake continues to bring good fishing to anglers today. It is especially noted for its good ice fishing. Lying close to Route 8 adjacent to Piseco Village, it is easily reached over well-plowed winter roads by a drive through the village to the back side of the lake. About 2.5 miles from the Route 8 turn to Piseco you will spot the fishing shanties. In any event, stop before you get to the Poplar Point State Campground. The best fishing is off that point. Adirondack ice fishing can be very cold but it can also be beautiful. A sunny winter afternoon on a snow-covered Adirondack lake, surrounded by mountain walls and good company, is truly an uplifting experience. Add to this image a twenty-two inch laker coming up through the ice and the picture is complete.

Piseco Lake is stocked with lake trout yearly. One of the recent stocking lists included 8,700 six-inch lake trout. A winter catch may include a mixture of stocked and native trout. The natives are darker with some white at the edges of the pectoral and vential fins. Stocked fish tend to have a more silvery color. Colors aside, it is one of the most delectable of the trout family.

Anglers who find Piseco Lake to be one of the best winter fishing lakes around know how to get those lakers. They follow the

The Great Southwestern Wilderness is for backpackers and boaters alike. Parts of this area are very remote and offer excellent trout fishing opportunities in a wild setting.

traditional ice fishing methods: tip-ups baited with minnows securely fastened in the back with small treble hooks. The springing up of a tip-up triggers the angler's adrenalin but a quick rush and a fast pull will lose the fish. The trick is to move slowly, let the hook set, and play the fish awhile. Caution pays off when a yellow-dotted laker is gently pulled through the open fish hole.

Piseco Lake is also a popular fishing lake during the warmer months. Good smallmouth bass fishing can be found in the north end of the lake. Stay near the middle and the west side; it is rocky near the island. Fishing off the weedy areas has also produced some bass for the summer fisherman. Whitefish, bullheads, perch and pickerel are other species caught during the summer months. There are three state campsites on the lake: Poplar Point, Point Comfort and Little Sand Point, with boat launching available at all three. Nearby hamlets can supply your needs and the adjacent mountains, streams and trails make it a great place to spend a fishing vacation.

Another good fishing bet in the southwestern Adirondacks is

West Canada Creek. Rising high in the Adirondacks, it is dammed by Hinckley Reservoir, and then meanders down to the Mohawk River.

West Canada Creek was once listed in a NYS publication as being near the top of the state's "Fishiest 50 " trout streams. Good trout fishermen agree. It can be fished successfully from beginning to end. Much of the best fishing is found near the bridges, the old bridge abutments near Poland, near fishermen's parking areas below Poland and above Middleville and the roadside fishing areas between Newport and Middleville. The biggest fish are taken in the spring, in the cold mountain waters above Hinckley. Good fish may be found near spring holes during the summer. The lower part of West Canada is discussed further in Ch. 12.

The upper reaches of West Canada are remote and are right in the heart of the Southwestern Wilderness. State land surrounds the South Branch, which flows roughly east to west and joins the main river at Nobleboro. The main branch goes northeast up through the town of Morehouse to the West Canada Lakes. Most of the main branch is surrounded by public lands. Fish the spots where feeder streams enter the main branch and fish up into some of the feeder streams. The riffle sections are usually productive. Minnows and worms work best in the deep pools during the early spring with flies, spinners, spoons, small plugs and worms in use as the water warms. The most popular fly seems to be the Royal Coachman. Phoebes and Mepps are popular spinning lures.

Move on, now, to try your luck in Limekiln Lake. It can be reached by taking Route 28 east from Utica, or Rt. 28 west from Blue Mountain Lake. Limekiln Lake is the western gateway for the Moose River Recreation Area. The entrance is reached by following a road running south and just east of the hamlet of Inlet.

Limekiln Lake is one of the cleanest bodies of water in the state. It is rated A —safe to drink—although all water should be purified before drinking. The 460-acre lake also holds an "A" trout rating. The number of fish a lake supports is stated in pounds per surface area, and at 100 pounds per surface acre we find

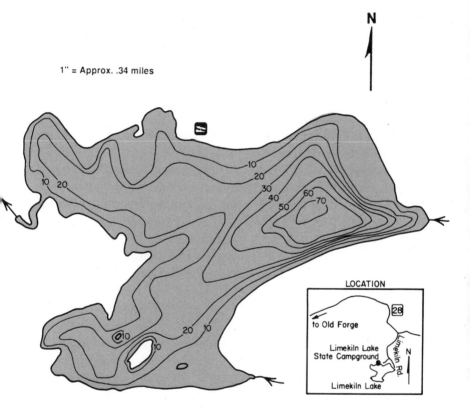

1" = Approx. .34 miles

N

LOCATION

to Old Forge

28

Limekiln Lake
State Campground

Limekiln Rd.

N

Limekiln Lake

Fig. 13.1 Limekiln Lake

that Limekiln Lake holds a good supply of fish. Limekiln Lake Campground offers a boat launch, so all of the fisherman's needs are present: a good lake, a supply of fish, nearby bait and tackle stores, a campground and a launching site.

Splake have been stocked in Limekiln Lake for many years. Those who like brook trout and lake trout will love splake fishing, since a splake is a cross between the two. The state record is over eleven pounds, taken from not-too-distant Eagle Lake ten years ago. A thirteen pounder was taken from the Adirondacks this past season but was not entered in the record books. It's just possible that a new record will be forthcoming. Regular catches range from two to eight pounds. The cove areas of Limekiln supply some of the best summer fishing.

Leaving Limekiln Lake we move into the Moose River Plains area, one of the wildest sections of the Adirondacks. Mostly state land, it abounds with fine fishing streams and ponds. The South Branch of the Moose River runs somewhat parallel to the southern side of the Moose River access road and the road crosses several feeder streams. Other streams and ponds in the area can be reached via an extensive trail system. Secondary roads and old log roads also run through the area providing additional access.

You may want to check the up-to-date regulations for the Moose River Recreation Area by getting the latest brochure from the Department of Environmental Conservation. No outboard motors are allowed, nor is the use of live baitfish. Other restrictions may also apply.

The Moose River was also in the Fishiest 50, a brochure DEC used to publish that listed New York State's top fifty trout streams. Besides the thirty-mile-long South Branch of the Moose River, there is also the North Branch which flows out of Big Moose Lake near Eagle Bay, and the Middle Branch near Old Forge. Depending on where you fish you may encounter brook, brown or rainbow trout. All sections have brook trout and the other species can be found from McKeever west. Once you are in the Moose River Plains, good fishing can be found almost anywhere.

It is not unusual to catch a limit in the main stream or by fishing up one of the feeder streams. You may take any size trout during the season, with the daily limit being ten.

The Cedar River Flow is the place to go if you own a small craft such as a pram, guideboat or canoe. It is a picturesque place to wile away your fishing hours and it is well-stocked with the New York State Fish, the brook trout.

The Cedar River Flow is the eastern gateway to the Moose River Wilderness. It is best reached by driving to Indian Lake on Route 30 and continuing through the village, crossing the Cedar River bridge and turning left at the next corner. You will see a cemetery on the left just before the turn. Proceed down the Cedar River road until you reach the end. You will find the Flow right at the entrance to the recreation area.

The Cedar River Flow is a great place to see trout feeding on flies and to try your luck at outsmarting them with some fly casting. Worms also work, though according to Izaac Walton, "Our hands have long been washed from the dirty things, satisfied not to fish when the fly cannot by used"! If you don't subscribe to this, know that mountain trout also love grasshoppers and crickets. If all else fails, try a kernel of corn or a piece of tomato. They work!

The time of day is important in fishing these Adirondack waters. During the early spring and late fall the trout feed during the middle of the day, especially when it is sunny. In the warm weather, trout are generally feeding during the morning and evening. In any case, watch closely for signs of surface feeding and you will multiply your chances for a successful catch. Fish the shores around the weeds when the Adirondack bugs are bouncing on the surface of the water.

For fishing such a large, remote area, you may want to give some thought to the hiring of a good fishing guide. Competent and reliable guides are available to make your trip safe and successful. Once the guide has shown you the fishing secrets in the Cedar River Flow, the West Canada Wilderness, or the Moose River Plains you can choose to go with or without a guide on your future trips.

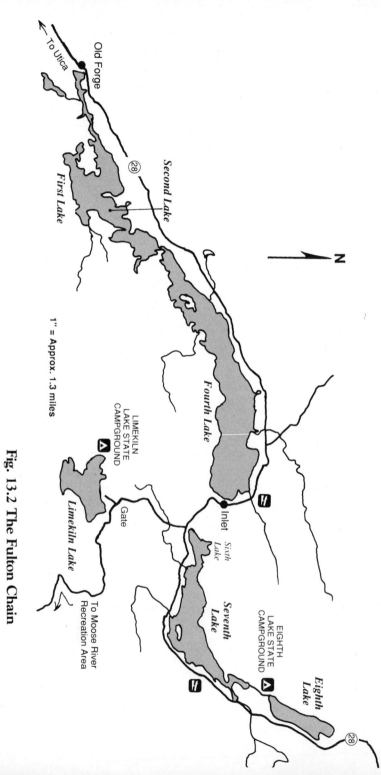

Fig. 13.2 The Fulton Chain

The Fulton Chain of Lakes on Route 28 have long been popular for fishing. First Lake can be found sprawling east from the village of Old Forge, fifty miles northeast of Utica. The eight lakes stretch northeast for some fifteen miles from that point almost to Raquette Lake. They can be seen and are easily reached from main highways. First, Second, and Third Lakes are closely connected by small passages. A longer, winding passage leads to the largest lake on the Fulton Chain, Fourth Lake. The hamlet of Inlet is at the head of Fourth Lake. Fifth Lake is a small pond not connected by passable waters to Sixth Lake. Seventh and Eighth Lakes are sizable lakes and along with Fourth Lake are popular fishing spots.

Fourth Lake is a good choice for a variety of fishing opportunities. Lake trout are taken in the spring along the shores, and from the middle of June on through the summer they are taken from the deeper waters. The deeper areas out from Eagle Bay and south of Cedar Island are good spots for trolling. Start the season with silver Rapalas and use some of your better "action" spoons later on.

Landlocked salmon, an introduced species, can be taken during the same time periods. In the early season, they are in the shallower areas especially where the feeder streams come in. Minnow-imitating lures and flies are used. Trolling throughout the summer pays off. Try trolling near the surface during the early morning in the roughly triangular area formed by Cedar Island, Dollar Island, and Inlet. A New York State boat launch is located at Inlet right on Route 28. A marina and boat launch can also be found in Inlet and a state launch site/picnic area is available at the end of Fourth Lake on South Shore Road.

Those who like shore fishing will find Fourth Lake a good bet during May. A big attraction is the rainbows which can be taken by casting from shore with live bait. A section near Route 28 just east of Barton Island holds good promise. Shore fishing can be practiced throughout the summer although trolling is the preferred method then. Add some "Christmas Trees" to your usual lures to attract the rainbows. The best spots are always near the islands.

Smallmouth bass are also present in Fourth Lake, with the best concentrations usually being found at the east end of the lake and in the small bays along the south shore. Evening fishing pays off when pursuing the smallmouths here. Popular lures such as Hula Poppers, Rapalas, and Mepps are put to work, and crabs (crawfish) and minnows are employed throughout the season.

Brown and brook trout are found at the west end of Fourth Lake near Alger Island. Spin casting with lures, fishing with live bait, and trolling with small plugs and spoons can all help to put a few browns and brookies in the frying pan.

Seventh Lake also has a convenient boat launch site on Route 28. The lake and the launch site are well marked and easily located. Seventh provides much the same fishing as Fourth Lake although it is not as large. NYS stocks Seventh Lake with rainbows, lakers, splake, and landlocked salmon. It is one of the best waters for splake fishing. Sixth Lake is also stocked with brook trout.

Eighth Lake is as popular as Fourth Lake in the Fulton Chain. The Eighth Lake Campsite, five miles west of Raquette Lake village, provides access and a place to stay. Eighth Lake is stocked with rainbows, lakers and landlocked salmon. Fishermen come from miles around to get those rainbows during the summer months. Getting an early start pays off and the best fishing spot is near the island in the east end. Trolling the section toward the highway with a Christmas Tree rig often attracts the rainbows that call Eighth Lake home.

One of the greatest outdoor experiences is to backpack and bushwhack into a remote pond for fishing. It is worth the effort whether you choose to rely on your own outdoor skills or play it safe with a guide. Backpack angling moves fishing one step further from the norm and provides a challenge for those with the gumption to try it.

There are 174 ponds in the southwestern Adirondack area and 88 of them hold a trout (T) designation. Study a topographical map and pick the one that looks best to you. The list would include three Beaver Ponds, six Buck Ponds, three Deer Ponds, four East Ponds, three Grass Ponds, six Mud Ponds, three Rock Ponds, and three Round Ponds—all rated for fish survival and/or trout. Some of the stocked ponds that you may see on the maps are Bear Pond, Bullhead Pond, Clear Pond, and Twin Pond. The complete list is available from DEC each year. Just pick a pond and make your plans.

How do we do it? We select the area we want to fish from a topographical map. For illustration let's pick the Old Forge Quadrangle. This Quadrangle is number G210 on the key to NYS topographical maps. This number is important in case the pond we pick is one of those several mentioned which share the same name. Fishing in the wrong pond could be an unsuccessful venture.

We may want to vacation and fish near the Fulton Chain of Lakes and also have access to the South Branch of the Moose River. We will make our base camp near Old Forge and locate a pond in that area for our fishing hike.

Bisby Road runs south out of Old Forge village to the Bisby Chain of lakes (another fishing possibility). Almost three miles out of the village the road crosses a trail that leads to Rock Pond at about the same spot it crosses the outlet of Little Moose Lake. Rock Pond is one of five waters by that name in the southwest Adirondacks. However, the one on this quadrangle is rated high for trout fishing.

The hike in to Rock Pond would take less than an hour and for those interested, another short hike would take them to some fishing on the South Branch of the Moose River. Those motivated for an extended backpacking trip could spend several days in this area trying out the fishing waters.

Other ponds can be found the same way. Another example might be a look at a reclaimed trout pond such as Jakes Pond in the Number Four quadrangle. Some ponds are more remote than these, but the fish are there for those who want to go after them. No one can guarantee a successful trip but the chances are multiplied when you get into the less fished waters of the southwest Adirondacks.

Don Williams is an Adirondack Guide, teacher, principal, and host of the TV program, "Inside the Blue Line." He grew up at the trailhead to the Northville-Lake Placid Trail. He serves as Adirondack Regional Editor for New York Sportsman, and has contributed articles to Adirondack Life and other publications. He has authored three books of local history, the latest being Oliver H. Whitman, Adirondack Guide. He resides in Gloversville with his wife Beverly. They have five grown children.

14

THE SECRET STREAMS
OF TUG HILL

by Allen Benas

Tug Hill is a large, elevated land mass located in the northern New York State counties of Lewis, Jefferson, Oneida and Oswego. While largely ignored by outside anglers, its 1,285,000 acres offer some of the best wilderness trout fishing opportunities in the state.

Although Tug Hill is little more than an hour drive from Utica, Syracuse and Watertown, it is time spent traveling back in history — back to the days when people were few, and the quiet remoteness of the surroundings made you wonder if anyone had ever stepped foot exactly where you were standing at the moment. This vast area, its silence interrupted only by the sounds of nature, is inspiring.

Today, Tug Hill is best known for receiving the greatest amount of snowfall east of the Rockies. Its average annual snowfall of 260 inches with a record of 355 inches (that's 29.6 feet!) in 1971 makes it a major source of water for the Black and Mohawk-Hudson River systems. Recreationally, this snowfall makes the Hill one of the most popular cross country skiing and snowmobiling areas in northern New York.

The area experienced its greatest population growth during the mid to late 1800's. Because it was a prime timber area, towns

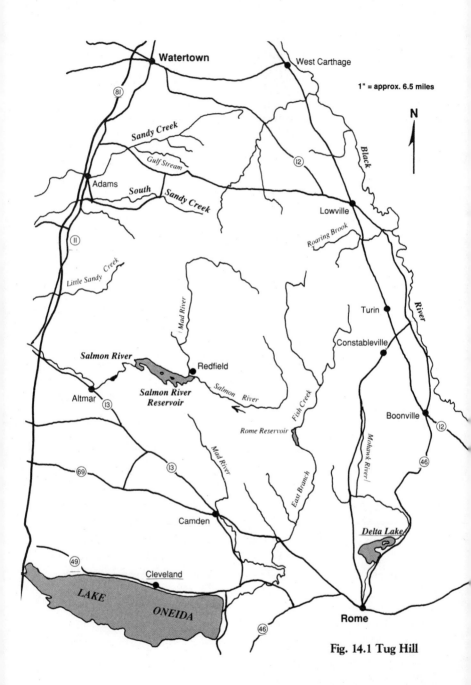

Fig. 14.1 Tug Hill

grew, new timber camps sprang up, and the railroad expanded its service area to haul the tons of spruce, hemlock and pines needed by the growing cities that surrounded it. The timber industry prospered until the early 1900's.

Agriculture followed the timber industry. However, farmers faced with the combination of short growing seasons and extreme amounts of precipitation found their efforts exhausting and often futile. The majority of farms were deserted by the 1940's and the land quickly reverted to a wilderness character. The demands put forth by nature bonded those who stayed on the Hill as it did their fellow frontiersmen who had moved west decades before. Those who live on the Hill today have retained this feeling of togetherness, and seem eager to extend their hands in friendship to those desirous of making the Hill a part of their lives.

Tug Hill trout streams reflect the region and range from small wild brook trout streams, to larger streams (such as the East and West Branches of Fish Creek, which support populations of wild and stocked brown trout as well as wild brook trout) to the lower Salmon River with large runs of steelhead, chinook and coho salmon. With this diversity of angling opportunity coupled with an array of streams too numerous to list, Tug Hill offers the trout hunter some fine fishing in a remote, uncrowded setting.

The headwaters of the Deer River, along with North and South Sandy Creeks, are located on the northern portion of Tug Hill in Jefferson and Lewis Counties. These streams are well known to local anglers for their excellent wild brook trout fishing, particularly during May and early June. The majority of fish are in the seven to ten inch size range, but brookies up to 15 inches are not uncommon. The best baits are worms or small spinners. Spinners are most effective when cast upstream and retrieved downstream slightly faster than the current. Some of the best streams are Raystone, Abijah, and the upper reaches of South Sandy Creek in the vicinity of Worth Center. South of the hamlet of Barnes Corners are the East and West Branches of the Deer River, the upper reaches of the Mad River, Edick Creek and Sears Pond. Also, North

Sandy Creek above the village of Adams is stocked with brown trout, and each spring holdover trout in the 15 to 17 inch size range are caught. These streams are generally small and brushy, and best fished with short fishing rods and hip boots. Since the best fishing coincides with the peak of the black fly season, a good supply of insect repellent is recommended.

The Salmon River watershed is located on the western slope of Tug Hill, primarily in Lewis and Oswego Counties, and flows westerly through Pulaski and enters Lake Ontario at Port Ontario. Above Redfield Reservoir, the East Branch of the Salmon is a high quality wild brown and brook trout stream. The brook trout generally range up to 12 inches and are abundant. Brown trout are found in the deeper pools, and DEC electrofishing surveys indicate that fish in the 15 to 20 inch size range are common. However, the browns are difficult to catch and best success is achieved by fishing early mornings or late evenings with large streamers or live bait.

These upper reaches of the salmon range in size from 20 to 50 feet wide, with pools in excess of four feet deep and a bottom of clean gravel. The water is gin clear and a careful approach improves fishing success. Summer dry fly fishing is at times outstanding.

The state has acquired over 20 miles of public fishing rights on the upper Salmon and its tributaries. Tributaries with public fishing rights that provide wild brook trout fishing are the lower Mad River, North Branch Salmon River, and Fall, Mallory, Stony and Prince Brooks. These streams are similar to those found on the north slope of Tug Hill and the same fishing techniques will prove effective.

Below Redfield Reservoir, the Salmon River supports the largest salmon and steelhead runs in the Lake Ontario drainage basin, providing year-round angling opportunities. Salmon in the 30-pound-plus size range and steelhead over 10 pounds are common. Effective techniques and angling locations vary with the seasons and timing of the runs. Current information can be obtained by calling the Oswego County Fishing Hotline (315-342-5873) or

Winter dies hard on Tug Hill. Often, deep snowbanks will greet you on April excursions to the rich trout waters of the Hill.

by contacting one of the numerous tackle shops in Pulaski. DEC's Salmon River fish hatchery is located on the river at Altmar, and is open to the public daily. The hatchery raises steelhead, chinook and coho salmon. *Great Fishing In Lake Ontario & Tributaries,* in this same series of books, covers the Salmon River in detail.

Between Lowville and Boonville in Lewis County a number of streams flow down the east slope of the Hill into the Black River. The character of these streams is markedly different from those just discussed. They are characterized by steeper gradients, small waterfalls and gorges, bedrock and broken rubble stream beds, and more variable seasonal flows. The upper reaches of these streams provide fishing for wild brook trout, while the lower portions are generally stocked with brook and brown trout. Wild browns are also present in a number of streams. Good fishing can be found throughout the season in the following: Roaring Brook, Whetstone Creek, Douglas Creek, Mill Creek (Turin), House Creek, the Sugar River and tributaries, and Mill Creek (Boonville).

These streams have generally good access, and can be fished

effectively with spinning and fly tackle. Fishing pressure is low, and it is not unusual to catch trout in the 12 to 15 inch size range. Whetstone Marsh Pond near the village of Martinsburg is stocked with tiger muskellunge and provides the unique opportunity to catch this hybrid cross of the muskellunge and northern pike. Tigers to 12 pounds are not uncommon here.

Undoubtedly the best trout fishing on Tug Hill is found on its south slope in the East and West Branches of Fish Creek located in southern Lewis and northern Oneida Counties. The Fish Creek watershed is large and both branches have numerous large and small tributaries. There are many road crossings and DEC has acquired approximately 55 miles of public fishing rights on the East Branch and its tributaries, and 28 miles on the West Branch system. In spite of the high fishing quality and excellent fisherman access, fishing pressure is generally light.

The Oneida County section of the East Branch from the village of Taberg upstream to Rome Reservoir is big water with fast runs and deep pools. Along with a wild brown and brook trout population, portions of the stream are stocked with yearling brown trout. The East Branch provides excellent fly fishing water. Large stonefly nymphs fished in the deeper runs in the early morning are particularly effective. Dry fly fishing is also good and there is usually a good green drake hatch in early June. This section is open to fishing until November 1, and spectacular catches can be made with minnows during late October, especially just below Rome Reservoir. Rome Reservoir itself is stocked with brown trout and fish up to four pounds are fairly common. Fishing is difficult due to the large minnow population in the reservoir.

Fishing pressure in the Lewis County section of the East Branch above Rome Reservoir is light, although fishing quality is excellent. The stream provides good fly, spin and bait fishing opportunities. A favorite section locally is off the Stinebricker Road in the town of Lewis. The East Branch has many excellent tributaries. Generally, all the smaller ones support populations of wild brook or brown trout. Some of the larger tribs that provide good fishing are

Furnace, Florence, Fall, Point Rock, and Alder Creeks. Besides wild trout, the lower reaches of each are stocked annually.

In contrast to the East Branch, the West Branch is generally a slow meandering stream, particularly above the village of Camden in Oneida County. It is floatable from the Westdale Dam in Oswego County downstream to Camden. The section is hard to fish, but can provide the determined angler with browns in the two to four pound size range. Live bait fishing is the most productive technique. Below Camden, the stream is similar to the East Branch, providing good fly and spin fishing for brown trout. Particularly good fishing can be found in the following tributaries: Little River, Mad River, Thompson Creek and Walker Brook.

At the confluence of the two branches at Blossvale, Fish Creek begins the transition from a cold to cool water stream. Smallmouth bass and walleye become more frequent, but large brown trout in the four to six pound range are regularly taken on live bait. A particularly productive area is off Passer Road in the town of Verona.

Three other overlooked streams originate on the south slope of the Hill. They are the East and West Branches of the Mohawk River, and the Lansingkill in the towns of Boonville, Ava, and Western in Oneida County. All three provide excellent fishing for wild and stocked brown and brook trout. The Lansingkill in the gorge between Boonville and Westernville is particularly good. Both branches of the Mohawk have relatively long, tough to reach sections that provide excellent fly fishing for brown trout in the 10 to 14 inch size range for those willing to walk.

By now it should be apparent that county highway maps or appropriate USGS quad maps are essential in finding the various streams and locations discussed. Highway maps can be purchased from the appropriate County Clerk's Office for a nominal fee. A key to the quad maps for New York can be obtained by writing to: Distribution Branch, United States Geological Survey, Box 25286, Federal Center, Denver, Colorado 80225 (tel. 303-236-7477). USGS maps can be ordered from this address or through many book and sporting goods stores. If you're in a hurry for

USGS maps, you can order them with a credit card number from Timely Discount Topos (800-821-7609), which for a modest surcharge will send them out quickly. Contour maps similar to (but with less color than) the USGS quads are published by the state and are available from: Map Information Unit, New York State Department of Transportation, State Campus, Bldg 4, Room 105, Albany, NY 12232 (518-457-3555).

The ambience of the Hill is not a state of mind, but very real. It offers an opportunity to relive what many consider the golden days of decades past...days when it was people against the elements throughout the year, and survival during the harsh winters was a daily chore. In truth, the type of experience that some anglers travel the world in search of can be enjoyed right here in this region of New York.

More in-depth information on Tug Hill is available from the Temporary State Commission on Tug Hill and the New York State Department of Environmental Conservation, both at the N.Y.S. Office Building, 317 Washington St., Watertown, N.Y., 1360l.

Allen Benas is a widely experienced St. Lawrence River fishing guide and resort owner. He writes actively about the outdoors and is a member of the Outdoor Writer's Association of America. Besides the St. Lawrence, he has fished and hunted farther afield, with the trout streams of Tug Hill being one of the places he dotes on.

15

BACK IN TIME ON THE OSWEGATCHIE

by Peter O'Shea

One of the most cherished adventures of early 20th century sportsmen, a canoe trek up the legendary Oswegatchie Inlet of Cranberry Lake in pursuit of its fabled brook trout, can still be had by modern anglers. The truly large brookies that once tempted the nation's fishermen and famed naturalists like Ernest Thompson Seton for the most part no longer exist. Much remains, though, not the least of which is the wilderness aura, one that increases as the distance from the launching site lengthens. Amid the beautiful surroundings, one can still thrill to the pursuit of the smaller trout that are present today, both in the Oswegatchie itself and in Cranberry Lake, the body of water it feeds.

Cranberry Lake is reached by proceeding west on Route 3 for 26 miles from the village of Tupper Lake to the hamlet of Cranberry Lake. Food and lodging are both available in the hamlet. A DEC campground is located just outside the village; turn south off Route 3 onto Lone Pine Road and go 1.3 miles to the campground entrance. It is usually open from Memorial Day through October. A bait and tackle shop is also located in the village.

Cranberry Lake itself, now approximately eleven square miles

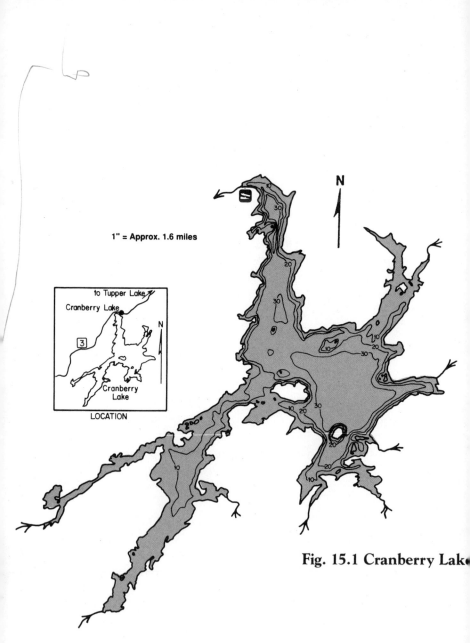

N

1" = Approx. 1.6 miles

to Tupper Lake
Cranberry Lake

3

Cranberry
Lake

LOCATION

N

Fig. 15.1 Cranberry Lake

in extent, doubled in size with the erection of a dam over a century ago. The dam flooded not only part of the Oswegatchie but also many of the lake's small feeder streams. These flooded inlets, or "flows," were once the place to fish for the lunker trout. The flooding also created a rather circular main body of water open to the west winds, and a series of shallow, sheltered inlets spiralling away like the spokes of a wheel.

The inadvertent introduction of yellow perch around 1945 led to the rapid demise of the renowned brook trout fishery. Smallmouth bass were introduced about 1960 and a fairly successful fishery for this species was established shortly thereafter. However in the late 1970's, acid rain began to lower the pH of the lake, and this led to a sharp reduction in the number of yellow perch. With the decline of this competing species, brook trout became re-established in Cranberry lake starting about 1980. The lake is now stocked regularly with brook trout and, in addition, there is some natural reproduction over the gravel beds of the river inlet in autumn. There still remains some fair fishing for smallmouth bass on occasion in the lake. Deep casting in the flows can be effective, especially in late July or August. Fishing the deeper waters off some of the lake's many islands can also prove rewarding at this time. Sears Island is one that comes to mind; try using live crayfish here.

Early in the year and during September, carefully fishing the shoals off the various flows will prove most productive. These shoal areas are marked by buoys in some cases.

Both Rapalas of different colors and live minnows have proven effective on smallmouth bass through the years on Cranberry. Rock bass of up to ½ pound are also present here, particularly in the flows. Besides worms, they are also susceptible to various small spinners. Dead Creek Flow is a good bet for both rock bass and the occasional lunker smallmouth bass. Smallmouth up to six pounds have been taken. Brook trout fishing in the main lake is also often best in the flows, particularly just after ice-out in early spring. The Cucumber Hole, one of the many bays of Dead Creek Flow, often proves rewarding for brook trout fanciers at this time.

Approximately 80% of the shoreline of Cranberry Lake is forest preserve as are a number of the many islands that dot the lake including Joe Indian, the largest. Designated sites have been assigned for primitive camping here by DEC. Boats may be launched from the DEC boat launching site located in the village on Columbian Rd. just south of Route 3.

The main feeder of Cranberry Lake is the Oswegatchie River. It flows approximately 26 miles through the boreal woodlands of the forest preserve from its source springs in a remote area south of High Falls to its mergence with the lake two miles below the hamlet of Wanakena. Except for a few short rapids in low water and one carry around a waterfall, the river is canoeable for 22 miles upstream from a public boat launching site at a non-inhabited place on the river called Inlet. See the accompanying map, Fig. 15.2.

Inlet, once the site of a sportsmen's hotel, is reached by turning south on a gravel road approximately one mile east of the village of Star Lake and heading south three miles through the forest preserve until the road terminates at a grassy parking area adjacent to a bend of the river. The two miles of the river below Inlet down to the hamlet of Wanakena are not canoeable but are stocked by

The location known as "Inlet" on the Oswegatchie. It's not a village, but rather a parking lot and official public launch and access point. Here, a group of Boy Scouts have just put in for an upriver journey.

DEC with brook trout. These miles can be fished successfully from the bank, especially where the river forms a pool. Fly fishing can be rewarding when the various mayfly hatches are swarming, which is often just before dark. The Royal Coachman is one dry fly frequently used here, while the Mickey Finn is a popular streamer pattern. Brown trout, too, are present in this two-mile stretch of river. In addition to offering exciting fly fishing opportunities, browns can also be fished with live minnows and with Rooster Tails, lures which seem to be especially favored locally. The red and white Daredevle is another lure that takes many brown trout here.

Before we talk about the most important part of the Oswegatchie, that section upstream of Inlet, a few words should be said about the river below Cranberry Lake.

Below the Cranberry Lake dam, the Oswegatchie flows through eight miles of a timber company tract that is leased to a sportsmen's club. An industrial dam erected still further downriver at Newton Falls has widened this stretch so that in most areas it resembles a shallow, marshy lake where nesting loons are present. Brook trout and brown trout are stocked annually here by DEC and are mostly found just below the dam at Cranberry Lake. Smallmouth bass and northern pike lurk in the wide, shallow areas where the water is warmer. Fishing is not prohibited in this stretch. The chief access is from a sandy ramp diagonally opposite the old Cranberry Lake dump on the Tooley Pond road, approximately .6 miles from its intersection with Route 3.

A canoe can be launched here and may be paddled for a number of miles downriver with a minimum of encumbrances. As the river meanders and widens, numerous weed beds are seen covering the shallows near the shore. A red and white Daredevle cast from a moving canoe or jon boat can often prove irresistible to northerns; 20 pounders have thrilled anglers here on occasion. The Rebel is another effective lure, and both of these lures can be used to good effect in late September and October as the fishing for northerns improves. Minnows or small yellow perch used in conjunction with a bobber usually bear fruit to varying degrees throughout the year. The smallmouth bass (along with some largemouth) present here are frequently taken with minnow-imitating lures.

The April 1 opening of the trout season is quite early for this northern clime. On this date, the lake itself is often still ice clad, while the river is still too cold and too high for the successful pursuit of trout. April 20 to May 1 is usually a more realistic time to begin fishing in this area.

Fishing the Oswegatchie by canoe is generally productive for brook trout for the whole distance of 22 miles above Inlet. At High Falls, a portage is necessary to gain access to the final seven miles.

As the canoe glides off from the sandy landing, a sense of tranquility is felt almost immediately. This reflects the fact that the Oswegatchie above Inlet is designated a "wild" river and, as such, motors of any kind are banned. During moderate to high water the few rapids encountered along the route are navigated fairly easily. At low water, mostly during the summer, a pole can come in handy. You start by paddling upriver against a normally gentle current. However, this current may increase for up to half a day after heavy rains. The trip downriver usually takes two thirds the time needed to paddle upstream.

The river meanders slowly, with frequent S-shaped curves giving the paddler ample time to both reflect on the beauty of the surroundings and to cast a worm or lure into the placid waters. (A lure frequently used here is the Panther Martin.) Fishing on the river early in the year can be quite fruitful in the pools lying at the feet of the several rapids. Heading upriver they are Griffin Rapids, Crooked Rapids, and the pool beneath High Falls. Worms and minnows are generally best at this time of year. The trout taken here, while generally small in size, are delicious and can offer a sporting battle.

During the summer when the water has warmed up considerably, by far the most productive places to cast a line are around the many "spring holes" encountered along the way. These are areas where a true spring bubbles up from the streambed or, more

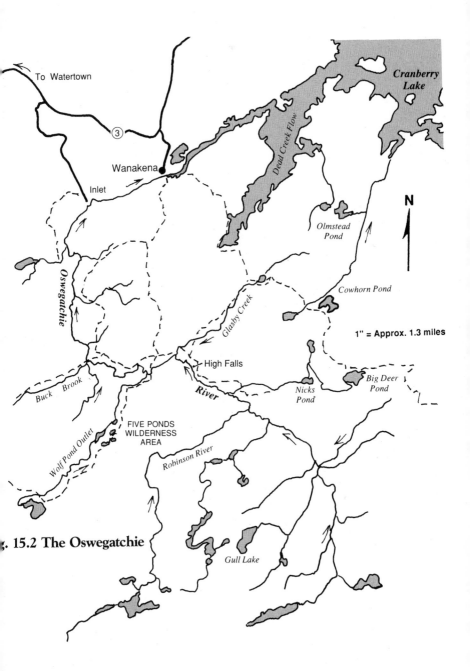

To Watertown

③

Wanakena

Inlet

Oswegatchie

Dead Creek Flow

Cranberry Lake

Olmstead Pond

N

Glasby Creek

Cowhorn Pond

1" = Approx. 1.3 miles

High Falls

Buck   Brook

River

Nicks Pond

Big Deer Pond

Wolf Pond Outlet

FIVE PONDS
WILDERNESS
AREA

Robinson River

. 15.2 The Oswegatchie

Gull Lake

often, where one of the many tributary streams enters the main river. The water stays cooler here during the summer and is far more attractive to trout during this season. These spring holes or tribs usually are named and well known locally. Going upriver you come across them as follows: Otter Creek, Dorset Creek, High Rock Creek, Cage Lake Springhole, Wolf Creek Springhole, and Carter's Landing Springhole. Worms and small minnows can still produce here even in summer, but spinners and other lures are utilized with increasing frequency as the summer progresses.

The river ambles on framed by an almost continuous canopy of balsam fir, tamarack, and white pine. The white pine in a few cases reaches heroic proportions, some trees exceeding 100 feet in height. After a mile, the river enters an open swamp where, amidst thick alders, two of the tributary creeks — Otter Creek on the right and Dorsey Creek on the left — add their measure to the Oswegatchie. These are traditional spring holes but will take some searching to discover as their entrances to the river are fairly well obscured.

After a short stretch in which the river straightens out, the Oswegatchie enters into a large boreal wetland for the next several miles. The river now meanders so extremely that local lore has it that an alert paddler can see the back of his neck. At 4.5 miles from Inlet, High Rock is reached. This is a huge boulder looking over the wide expanse of wetland just passed through. Primitive camping facilities including a privy are located at High Rock; a trail leads from here out to the village of Wanakena in four miles. Tiny High Rock Creek comes in here also. It is another of the more prominent spring holes along the river. It was near this spot in 1982 that two DEC forest rangers saw a cow moose and her calf swim across the river, the first indication of breeding success for moose to emerge in over 100 years in the Adirondacks.

It would be well to mention here that the sights and delights of wildlife add immeasurably to the enjoyment of the entire trip along the river. While there are rivers in the Adirondacks that outstrip the Oswegatchie in the output of trout, few areas surpass it insofar as the quality of wildlife observed and of the wilderness encountered. Therein may lie the ultimate attraction of this small river. Osprey frequently hunt over the river, and often they can be seen plunging in after fish (hopefully not trout!) Loons are often heard, but their calling is from one of the nearby interior ponds as the river itself is too narrow to accommodate them, being only 75 feet at its widest point near Inlet. Broods of mergansers and black ducks are also commonly seen on the river, while great blue herons hunt for frogs in the shallows all along the river's course.

Beaver are abundant on the river and many times can be seen swimming alongside the canoe as dusk approaches. Their dams are not much in evidence as they most often utilize bank dens along the river, especially below High Falls. Otter are also very numerous. They occasionally can be observed sticking their head above the water like a seal, but more often their sign in the form of slides and rolling areas will be noticed in grassy areas on the shore. Whitetail deer are more common here than in many other areas of the Adirondacks. They can frequently be seen feeding on the shores and the stretch of the river from the "plains" to High Falls is a large winter deer yard. These upper Oswegatchie deer are notable both for their size and the imposing girth of many of their racks. Black bear, too, are quite common along the entire length of the river and they will occasionally be sighted. Much more often they will make their presence known as they forage for food around the campsite at night. A safety rule when camping along the river at night is to make sure that all food items are tied high out of the reach of hungry bears, and definitely out of the tents.

A short ways upstream from High Rock the river leaves the wide marsh and enters a long, narrow, relatively straight corridor called the Straight of the Woods. The banks are lined here with the cathedral-like spires of balsam fir until the next prominent spring hole is reached, Griffin Rapids, 6.5 miles above Inlet. A DEC lean-to is located here and the first parcel of unharvested or "old growth" forest is seen on the river bank. This magnificent stand of sugar maple and beech with an occasional venerable hemlock extends all the way to Buck Pond. The rapids, which are hardly noticeable in medium to high water, provide good fishing (at their heads and also in the pools below) for brook trout of up to 12 inches.

Approximately 8.5 miles above Inlet is Cage Lake spring hole. A foot bridge spanning the river, and a marked trail going to Buck Pond and Cage Lake previously existed here but were recently abandoned by DEC due to the repeated washing out of the bridge in spring floods and to incessant beaver flooding of the hiking trail. In addition to currently being the site of an excellent spring hole, the area is also the site of another DEC lean-to. As with all the lean-tos along the Oswegatchie, there is a noticeable paucity of firewood in the immediate vicinity.

Taking off again, the paddler next comes to an imposing stand of large white pine and tamarack lining the river approximately 12 miles above Inlet. The scenery here is, in many respects, more reminiscent of Alaska than New York State. At 12.5 miles the one foot bridge still remaining above Inlet is encountered. Crossing the river here is the Five Ponds Trail, which takes you to remote Sand Lake after another 8.5 miles of hiking. On the way this trail passes the entrancing Five Ponds themselves, from which the entire Oswegatchie wilderness takes its name. In the vicinity of the five tiny ponds stands a group of magnificent virgin red spruce.

Wolf Creek Outlet is next. This spring hole has produced trout since the days of the early Adirondack guides who had rustic camps in the vicinity. After that, Round Hill Rapids is the next major feature. It and Ross Rapids a little farther upriver are two of the more difficult rapids and in low water a short carry may be necessary. Fishing for brook trout with worms or minnows at the foot of the rapids is productive during early spring. Another mile on, or about 14 miles upstream of Inlet, yet another notable spring hole is reached: Carter spring hole. This name refers to the area between Glasby Creek and Moses Rock Spring, an interval of roughly 100 yards. Glasby Creek drains that unique area known as the "Plains," a large open area in a region of otherwise uninterrupted forests. The plains, which covered the valley between Round Top Mountain and Three Mile Mountain, have only recently begun to revert to forest: black cherry, balsam fir, and tamarack. The Plains, however, retain a generally semi-open aspect.

Finally, 15 miles from Inlet, High Falls is reached. At the foot of the rapids extending from the Falls there exists one of the river's traditional fishing hot spots. The Falls have been a prime wilderness destination for nearly a century going back to the era of Dobson's camps, a popular rustic lodge catering to sportsmen. Nestled under handsome white pine and hemlocks, two other DEC lean-tos are located on either side of the river. Several popular, marked hiking trails also converge here.

Immediately above the Falls (after a short carry) the river changes character becoming more narrow with a deeper channel. The trout get smaller but are still present. More of the trout are now of the native strain, distinguished by salmon-colored flesh, and are excellent eating. On occasion, fly fishing can be quite exciting above the Falls. Fishing into the current is best, and remember that the main hatches of mayflies and stoneflies occur here from 10 to 20 days after the hatches in the southern part of New York State due to the cooler weather. The Black Gnat is one fly to consider using here. At the confluence of the Oswegatchie and the Robinson Rivers, approximately three miles above High Falls, good fishing is provided by the food washed into the Oswegatchie by the Robinson. Like the spring holes below the Falls, fishing in the pool here remains rewarding throughout the summer. The head of navigation is about six or seven miles above the Falls depending on water levels. It is approximately 3.1 miles to the junction of the Robinson River with two notable spring holes in between Nick's Pond outlet and Red Horn Creek.

After two miles of paddling, you see a ridge with very large pine on the left. This is known as Pine Ridge and it is an authentic stand of "old growth." It was known as the finest example of virgin white pine in the entire eastern United States before the entire area was decimated by the blow-down of 1950. What remains is still impressive. The best way to see it is to ascend the ridge on an unmarked trail that takes off from an open grassy area on the shore known as Camp Johnny. Camp Johnny is one of the historic primitive camp-sites that are located along the river, and which are available for public camping for up to three days without a permit.

The Robinson River descends to meet the Oswegatchie next, coming in on a series of rapids approximately a mile after Camp Johnny. Above here the going gets more difficult as the route of the river becomes encumbered with numerous beaver dams and blow-downs. Although the Robinson River is the last traditional spring hole, many small brook trout are still to be found upriv-er. Fishing for them can be a little difficult with the many alders arching over the river. The trout here are probably best fished for from the many beaver dams that now span the river. This same situation prevails along the lower reaches in areas where small spring creeks enter the Oswegatchie. In many instances the beaver have chosen the exact location where the bodies of water meet to erect the dam and fishing the pool created by this dam is often good.

Several miles above the Robinson River the Oswegatchie fans out into various separate feeder creeks and becomes basically unnavigable. Again, though, many of these feeders can be ascend-ed for various lengths depending on water levels. At one time, the pond created by the huge beaver dam near the junction of these feeders was a mecca that beckoned trout fishermen from far and wide. There is still some good trout fishing present here today.

This concludes the Oswegatchie sojourn upriver. The trip down-river will definitely be quicker, and may even reveal some Oswegatchie gems that remained hidden on the upstream paddle.

There remains one final fishing opportunity in this fascinating area — the beckoning of the remote, headwater ponds. Pursu-ing the wily trout in these forest-clad bodies of water offers perhaps the zenith in true wilderness fishing. Nestled deep in the forest preserve, they are reached only after long hikes on DEC marked trails. The way is arduous as the ponds are best fished by boat and the trek in will usually involve taking a lightweight canoe. No matter. Many consider it worthwhile, both for the tranquility earned and the splendor of the majestic forest travelled through. The difficulty here only enhances the wilderness experience.

Acid rain has affected these interior ponds more than it has Cranberry Lake or the Oswegatchie River. (See the discussion in the front of this book.) Those ponds with natural buffering ability have fared best. A number have also been temporarily improved by liming. Most suitable ones have been aerially stocked with brook trout by DEC. Some large trout are still present in these ponds and are best caught by trolling or fly fishing. Trolling is most productive in early spring, and many trollers favor lures with a worm trailing behind. During warmer weather, the areas of natural springs will have to be sought. The trout will be found congregating there. While increasing acidity has limited the percentage of juvenile fish surviving, three and even four pound trout are still present in some of these waters as ample reward for the energetic angler who undertakes the long hike back to them.

Following are a sample of some of the ponds that are still moderately productive. While there are others, these will serve quite well as an introduction:

COWHORN POND. This 21 acre pond is reached by a hike of 6.5 miles from a trailhead in the hamlet of Wanakena, or, alternatively, a 4.1 mile trail from the southwest bay of Cranberry Lake which can be reached via motor boat.

DARNING NEEDLE POND. This 30 acre pond can be reached only by a 2.6 mile hike on a trail taking off from the southeast bay of Cranberry Lake. This trip can be done in combination with a day's fishing on Cranberry Lake.

TAMARACK POND. Comprising 13 acres, this pond is reached by a hike of 8.4 miles from the hamlet of Wanakena over the same trail used to reach Cowhorn Pond. In addition, the same alternative exists as at Cowhorn, a six mile hike from the trailhead on the southwest bay of Cranberry Lake.

HEDGEHOG POND. This approximately ten acre pond can

be reached after a short ½ mile hike on a trail from the west shore of Cranberry Lake.

Other interior ponds productive for brook trout include Olmstead Pond, the beautiful Five Ponds, and fabled Cage Lake. Cage is reached only after a nine mile trek from the village of Star Lake or an almost equally lengthy hike from the Oswegatchie River along the marked Five Ponds trail.

A retired police officer, Peter O'Shea is now a naturalist and writer living in New York's St. Lawrence County. He has canoed, trekked and fished all around the Oswegatchie wilderness country. He is also keenly interested in hunting and cross country skiing. Peter is the author of several books on hiking in the northern Adirondacks and, in addition, has contributed to a number of magazines. He is a member of the Wildlife Society, the Adirondack Mountain Club and other groups.

16

HIGHWAY THROUGH
THE MOUNTAINS

by Tony C. Zappia

Stretching from Raquette Lake in central Hamilton County all the way north to its confluence with the St. Lawrence river east of Massena, the Raquette River offers a high-quality and varied outdoor experience. From large, crystal clear mountain lakes to numerous white water rapids and easy flowing stretches of river, the Raquette is readily accessible by motor vehicle yet remote enough to set the stage for a true angling odyssey.

The Raquette undergoes several changes from lake to river along its course. Let's begin our discussion with Raquette Lake, its source.

Raquette Lake's physical features are impressive. It stretches over five miles in length and three miles in width, and has a maximum depth of 96 feet. At 5,274 acres, Raquette is the eighth largest lake in the Adirondacks. It has 99 miles of shoreline, and numerous points, inlets and islands.

As soon as ice-out occurs, brook trout fishing from shore along Rt. 28 is often very good. Worms seem to be the brookies' favorite meal this time of year and fish over two pounds are annually weighed in at nearby bait and tackle stores. When the weather warms, brookies will move deeper and may be found near spring holes and cold tributaries.

The second trout (really a char) indigenous to Raquette Lake is important throughout the Adirondacks: the lake trout. Raquette Lake lakers serve as brood stock insofar as they supply eggs for the Chateaugay Fish Hatchery. At the same time, DEC annually stocks the lake with approximately 8,400 yearling lakers.

A boat is required to fish for lake trout. In the spring, they can be taken in 30-50 feet of water by trolling flutter spoons with lead core line or copper wire. Downriggers are also used for deep trolling and lighter line can be utilized. When concentrating on lakers, it is most important to fish the bottom and fish it slow. Midday (between 10 A.M. to 2 P.M.) often produces the most fish.

As the water warms, lakers find their way to the deeper parts of the lake. At this time, trollers look to the north end where maximum depth reaches 96 feet. The majority of fish will be found in 35-60 feet, and a depth finder would certainly come in handy to locate fish on bottom near structure or occasionally, suspended.

As winter sets in, ice fishing with smelt or suckers will generate good catches. Both the north and south ends are favored locales for hard water lakers.

Bass occupy a different niche here, and they are extremely plentiful. Although bass fishing can be good throughout the summer, Labor Day signals the beginning of cool weather and the best bass fishing period. Smallmouths and largemouths begin to feed heavily and respond well to bait and lures. Both largemouths and smallmouths congregate along weed beds scattered along the lake, so look for deep water drop-offs that border these weed beds and drop your offerings into 10 to 18 feet of water. Minnows and crawfish are the number one and two baits. As for lures, Mr. Twisters, Rapalas and top water lures such as the Zara Spook, buzzbaits, Jitterbug, Hula Popper and smaller fly rod poppers can all produce.

While bass and trout fishing may be more exciting, nothing will fill the freezer faster than a couple of days of perch and bullhead fishing. Bullhead can be taken from shore in early spring and fall by fishing mud bottom in 5 to 15 feet of water. Where you find lilypads along bays, you will usually find perch. Anglers need to offer worms to both perch and bullhead. Under the ice, perch will take a small minnow.

A small boat or canoe is not needed to take pailsfull of bullhead or perch, but for trout and bass fishing a small to medium sized boat is required. A 12-16 foot aluminum or fiberglass shallow V-hull is ideal; the motor should be no smaller than 9.9 h.p. Boat launching facilities are scattered throughout the town of Raquette Lake. Along Route 28 there are four boat launches that will adequately handle a good-sized craft. Most marinas along the lake will serve the majority of your needs from bait to boating supplies.

Only ¼ mile from Raquette Lake, and part of the same river system, Forked Lake is a medium-sized Adirondack lake spanning 1,248 acres and with a maximum depth of 74 feet. Quite rocky, this lake offers both largemouth and smallmouth bass, as well as a good population of brook trout. Both perch and sunfish please the shoreline angler through those hot summer days.

But before the summer doldrums set in, brook trout can be taken in the Raquette River between Raquette Lake and Forked Lake as well as in the waters between Forked Lake and Buttermilk Falls. A three mile section above Buttermilk Falls is annually stocked with 2,500 yearling brookies during the spring. Spinners, worms, streamers and the ever popular gold Pheobe will help you fill the frying pan during those cool spring days.

As the days get warmer, brookies will move toward the northwestern part of Forked Lake. Here they will lie in deep holes during the day and move up to the surface at night to take a dry fly, either a real one or one with a hook in it.

Since Forked Lake contains so many rocky shoals and points, the smallmouth bass thrive and many push the scales to the four pound mark. Smallies can be found early in the year along shallow rocky areas with weed beds. It seems as though the fish tend to favor the eastern end of the lake, especially near the outlet waters and near the state campground.

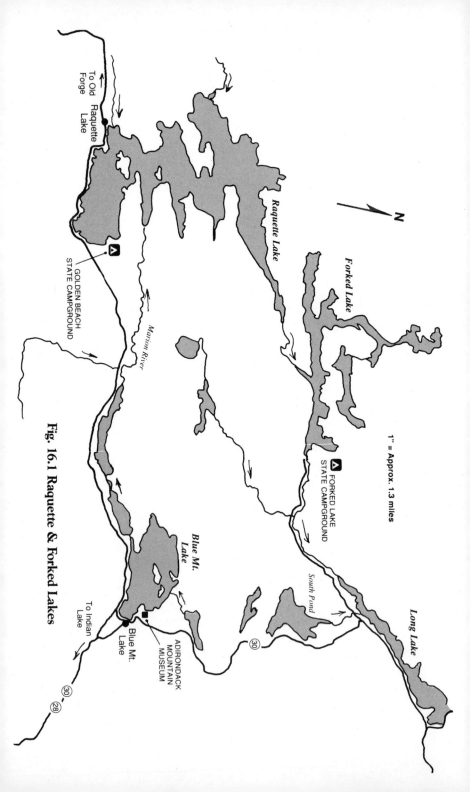

Fig. 16.1 Raquette & Forked Lakes

Largemouth bass do well in these waters. Plenty of weed cover offers old bucketmouth plenty of prime locations from which to launch an ambush. To successfully fish largemouths in Forked Lake, one should try rubber worms, spinnerbaits, Mr. Twisters and various top-water lures. Best bets for locating largemouth are along the east end where a rock ledge and weed bed are present. Shallow bays make up the west end of the lake, and largemouth are consistently taken here.

The only effective way to fish for bass in Forked Lake is out of a boat. Since the lake is relatively shallow, a boat rigged with an engine larger than four or five H.P. would be impractical. Most anglers prefer to use 16-foot canoes or small flatbottom jon boats. At the Forked Lake Public Campground, anglers can launch a boat and park for $2.50/day while the 78 campsites surrounding the lake cost $6/night. The campsites are on a first come, first served basis.

Caution: Forked Lake runs west to east and during strong west winds can become quite dangerous for canoeists and others using small craft.

For those who choose to paddle their way from Forked Lake to Long Lake, the Raquette River drops 116 feet in five miles and three carries must be made to reach the base of Buttermilk Falls. During the spring, brook trout can be taken by fishing at the mouths of feeder streams where they form the Raquette. Worms and spinners work well, but the current will be fairly swift and pools and eddies will yield the most fish. Canoeists are warned that the rapids above and below Buttermilk Falls are extremely dangerous during high water, and Buttermilk Falls is not runable.

The falls can be reached by motor vehicle from the village of Long Lake by traveling south on Routes 28N/30 and turning right onto North Point Road. Buttermilk Falls parking area is located on the right side of the road and is approximately 5.5 miles from the center of Long Lake.

Anglers fishing out of canoes can resume their journey through the Raquette river system about .25 miles from the base of Buttermilk Falls. The 4.5 mile section of water upriver of the village of Long Lake is scattered with shallow bays of pickerelweed and pond lilies which are home to the great northern pike and both

A sign at the official access/launch area at the southern end of Long Lake. This lake is often part of a Raquette River tour. It can also be used as access to the Cold River and some wilderness trout fishing.

smallmouth and largemouth bass. Fishermen who have smaller motorboats in the 14-18 foot class can launch at the state boat ramp, Town Dock Road, approximately ½ mile from Long Lake Town Beach. Also, there are many private marinas with boat launches along Long Lake, and a minimal launch fee will be charged. For the angler without a boat, several places in Long Lake will rent small boats for this purpose.

Long Lake is a fairly shallow, 14-mile-long lake with a maximum depth of 45 feet. Located in northeastern Hamilton County between Routes 28N and 30, the lake is essentially a widening of the Raquette River. It flows roughly south to north, and prevailing summer winds favor downlake travel (south to north).

Northern pike are abundant in Long Lake. Their average weight is three to four pounds, although pike in the 10 to 15 pound class can be taken. One of the best areas on the lake for northerns is a place called Big Marsh. Located about 2.5 miles north of the village, Big Marsh lies on the western shoreline directly across from Catlin Bay, and is defined by a series of marker buoys. Fishermen here cast Daredevles and sinking Rapalas, and use live bait early in the morning and later on in the evening. As the water warms, pike will migrate out into the deeper water and anglers will find them in 15 to 30 feet. Other hotspots for northerns on Long Lake are the western bays just south of the Long Lake Route 30 bridge and the north marsh at the very foot of Long Lake.

Along the north marsh, smallmouth and largemouth bass are concentrated. Since the lake is shallow, the warming of the water tends to play a critical role in fish behavior. Bigger fish will feed heavily at night and in early morning, and fishing Long Lake during midday is generally a waste of time. The only exception is during pre-spawn conditions. At these times in spring, both pike and bass can be caught any time of day by casting top-water lures close into shore, especially in shallow sandy or weed-filled areas.

When summer arrives, try the deep hole located at the north end of the lake. This 45-foot fish holding area will produce large northerns and bass trying to escape the tepid water temperatures associated with a shallow lake. Recently, a dead pike was discovered floating on top of the water near that area. The fish weighed in at 18 pounds 12 ounces. If you have a boat equipped with a depth finder, look for suspended fish over deep areas and vertically jig for them. During the early morning and evening hours, concentrate your fishing along structure, such as islands, located adjacent to the 45 foot hole.

Pan fishermen can experience reasonably good perch and bullhead action just about anywhere in the lake. Most panfishing activity occurs around Big Marsh.

Marinas, hotels, stores and restaurants are primarily located along the eastern shoreline. The south end of the lake is considerably developed while the north end is mostly Forest Preserve.

The distance from the village of Long Lake to the north end is 9.5 miles. While traveling downlake, you will see lean-tos scattered along the eastern shoreline that are available for use. During peak summer months, lean-tos will become less available due to the hundreds of canoeists traveling through the Raquette River system. If you plan on spending a few days and nights fishing the north end, it would be advisable to carry along a tent.

Let's continue our journey northward on the Raquette. As the river flows out of Long Lake, it forms a marsh which empties into a slow winding network of islands and sandbars. A canoe or small motorboat can make its way through this six-mile long, slow moving section of stream until the hills close in as you approach Raquette Falls. You must make a 1.3 mile carry here in order to continue downstream.

Below (downstream of) the falls, pan-sized brown trout can be taken using worms, spinners and various fly patterns. Each year, DEC stocks a one mile stretch at Raquette Falls with 1,200 yearling brown trout. This annual stocking currently takes place by air.

As the river descends some 80 feet, plunging over a rocky bed, the heavy rapids aerate the warm water at the base of the falls. This highly oxygenated water draws both cold and cool water species of fish. Your first cast with a crawfish can take a two pound brown while your second cast can produce a 24-inch walleye.

The base of Raquette Falls is extremely productive for northern pike and smallmouth. Walleye averaging 18-24 inches during the spring also find their way to the base of the falls. Both pre- and post-spawn walleyes can be tangled with here. Sinking Rapalas, deep diving crankbaits, spinner/worm combos or crawfish can draw good responses.

Still paddling downstream, we come to where the Raquette empties into Tupper Lake, discussed in Ch. 6. As we leave Tupper Lake and head west on Route 3, we arrive at Piercefield about seven miles later. Now fully harnessed for generation of hydroelectric power, the river from Piercefield Flow to Raymondville (65 miles downstream) is host to 20 dams and has been nicknamed the "Workhorse River of the North." In spite of this great human intrusion on the lower Raquette, certain fishing opportunities have been created.

Piercefield Flow, the uppermost impoundment on this section

of the Raquette, offers fishing opportunities in a pond-like situation. Anglers can take northern pike, smallmouth bass, an occasional walleye and a variety of panfish. Below Piercefield and downstream to Carry Falls Reservoir is a very wild stretch of the Raquette, one that provides good fishing for smallmouth bass. Although presently used as a canoe route by white water enthusiasts, the surrounding land is almost entirely private and access

Walleyes, like this one of trophy size, are an important part of the menu of a Raquette River float-to-fish trip.

is limited. DEC is presently negotiating to obtain public access along this stretch, but for now, portages around rapids and falls are on private land.

For the next 27 miles, beginning with Carry Falls Reservoir, the Raquette is no longer a river; rather, it is a series of eight reservoirs ranging in size from 122 to thousands of acres. Boat launch sites and campgrounds can all be found here. While it varies from reservoir to reservoir, angling is generally good. Walleye, northern pike, yellow perch, smallmouth bass, bullhead and a variety of other panfish can all be taken in this stretch.

The largest of the reservoirs, Carry Falls — the fifth largest lake in the Adirondacks — is located on Route 56 about three miles north of Sevey Corners. A blacktop road of .7 miles connects this 6.6 mile long reservoir with Route 56.

The Parmenter Campsite here offers fishermen overnight sites for tents or trailers, picnic tables, toilet facilities, drinking water and fireplaces. The fee is minimal, and there is no charge for parking or day use.

After camp has been set, you may want to check on water conditions. Water levels can fluctuate as much as 20 feet in Carry Falls, and this will determine the day's fishing activities. As a rule, maximum water level occurs in late April through June, while minimum levels are encountered by late September.

Walleye are the favorite fish, and most anglers troll very slowly with a spinner/worm harness. This is tied to a three-way swivel with either one or two ounces of weight attached to the system enabling the rig to bounce bottom. While trolling for walleye it is common to hook into large yellow perch. These tasty fish can reach the two pound mark and are abundant here.

The head of Carry Falls Reservoir seems to be a favorite spot with fishermen. Much activity occurs just below the rapids where water is rich in oxygen and a bit cooler. Early morning and late evening should prove most productive.

Both spring and fall tend to produce the biggest stringers. There are large northern pike cruising the reservoir, so be prepared for bite-offs while fishing for walleye and perch. If you're out after northerns make sure you spool up with at least 12 pound line, and if possible, tie on a heavier mono or wire leader for extra measure.

A word of advice from an old pro who fishes Carry Falls Reservoir: When trolling for walleye, make certain that you troll into the sun for best daytime results.

The final 63 miles of the Raquette winds its way through south-

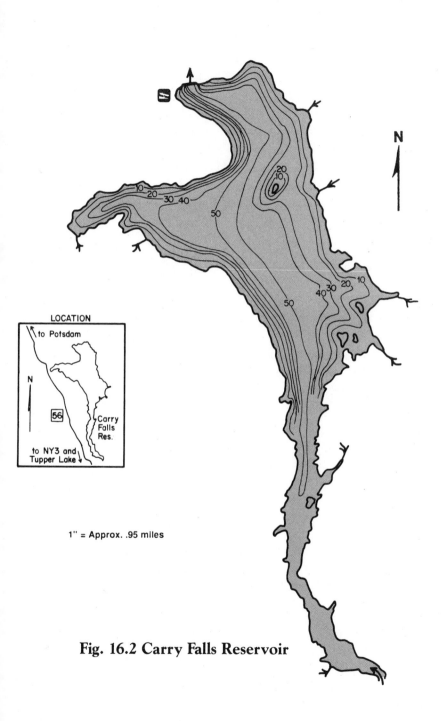

Fig. 16.2 Carry Falls Reservoir

LOCATION

to Potsdam

N

56

Carry
Falls
Res.

to NY3 and
Tupper Lake

1" = Approx. .95 miles

N

10 20 30 40

50

20
10

40 30 20 10

50

central St. Lawrence County. It is still flowing essentially north-ward. The stretch of river from Raymondville to Massena produces good catches of smallmouth bass and walleye. Also, the occasional St. Lawrence River muskellunge can be boated during late spring and fall.

Like an old back country road winding its way through the mountains, bending to the left and then to the right, descending down a sloping, hilly, mountain pasture scattered with wild-flowers, the Raquette River traverses more than a hundred miles of the beautiful Adirondack Region. For fishermen and other outdoor lovers, it is truly a highway through the mountains.

Tony C. Zappia was born and raised in Massena, New York. He has served as Editor for Northern Tier Sportsman *and is currently a free-lance outdoor writer/photographer and Outdoor Editor for the* Watertown Daily Times. *He is a member of the Outdoor Writer's Association of America, the NYS Outdoor Writers Association and other groups.*

17

FISHING POLE, PADDLE
AND PORTAGE
by Joe Hackett

The St. Regis Canoe Area is one of the finest places in the Adirondacks to canoe and fish. Located north of the old Remsen-Lake Placid railroad tracks between Paul Smiths and Upper Saranac Lake, the area consists of 58 ponds and lakes, all located on or around the three streams that eventually combine to form the northward flowing St. Regis River. Within the St. Regis Canoe Area, which is state land open to all, motors of any kind are forbidden. There are several entrances to the area, all of which require portages. Once into the area, a canoeing angler has literally dozens of options in planning a specific itinerary.

There are two public boat launch/parking areas at the eastern end of the St. Regis Canoe Area. One is located on Little Clear Pond, behind the Saranac Inn State Fish Hatchery off Rt. 30; no fishing is allowed in Little Clear Pond as it is a brood pond for landlocked salmon. Access to St. Regis Pond, the largest pond in the area, is made via a two mile paddle up Little Clear Pond then a quarter mile carry. The other launching site is located off Rt. 30 on Upper St. Regis Lake, next to the private Lake Shore Owners Association's boathouse and docks. This site requires a half mile paddle across the Upper St. Regis Lake and several short carries through Bog Pond, Bear Pond, and Little Long Pond.

The western end of the St. Regis Canoe Area is accessible off the Floodwood Road, four miles west of the state hatchery on Rt. 30. The Floodwood Road divides the St. Regis Canoe Area from the Fish Creek–Rollins Pond Camping Areas. It is also the dividing line between cold water and cool water gamefish species. For access to this section of the St. Regis Canoe Area, a state launch is located on Hoel Pond, adjacent to the Saranac Inn Golf Course. Putting in on Hoel Pond requires a paddle of two miles across the pond, a carry over the railroad tracks and into Turtle Pond. From Turtle Pond, one can paddle into Slang Pond and carry over to Long Pond or carry one mile into Clamshell Pond directly. From Clamshell, a half mile carry leads to Fish Pond. Long Pond, which has a state launch on its western end, can be accessed via the Floodwood Road just past the West Pine Pond turnoff. Long Pond has a decent population of smallmouth bass and is a starting point for trips to Ledge Pond, which holds lake trout, brook trout and lots of perch. Also accessible from Long Pond are carries to Mountain Pond (brook trout) and the trail to Nellie and Bessie Ponds, which requires a mile long carry. Fishing the ledges along the narrows on Long Pond always produces some nice smallmouth bass.

Now that you know where to go, let's discuss why you should go. The ponds and lakes of the St. Regis Canoe Area were scooped out by glaciers and they lie very close together. Most portages are no more than one hundred yards and are well maintained by the DEC. All are marked by small white directional signs, and you can easily travel from pond to pond and fish several ponds each day from a base camp. This is the most effective method as it allows a fisherman a chance to find which pond is producing on which particular day. Travel in the St. Regis Canoe Area speaks well to the value of a lightweight canoe, and the Kevlar models are the finest. Tugging a heavy aluminum or ABS canoe over a one-mile-long, buggy, muddy carry is not my idea of a good time. Be sure to travel light, with canoe and gear.

The St. Regis Canoe Area can be best described in two sections, the East End and the West End.

The East End is centered around St. Regis Pond. It holds a good population of lake trout (18 inch minimum size limit), splake and brook trout. It is best fished on calm days, as the wind can make for rough water due to the size of the pond. Trolling shorelines or casting spinners along the shore of the big island on St. Regis Pond is a good bet in the early season. As the heat of the summer intensifies, fish deep using copper or lead core line about 50 yards off the island. The East End of the canoe area also holds Little Long Pond, Grass Pond, Little Clear Pond (no fishing), Bear Pond, Bog Pond, Ochre Pond, Green Pond, Meadow Pond and St. Germain Pond. Nearly all of these little jewels hold brook trout, some lake trout, splake and rainbows. Little Long Pond is well known for its splake and rainbows. Fly hatches are common in these stone bottom ponds and are very noticeable on

Canoeing in to fish the St. Regis area is one of the most popular Adirondack trips. There are literally dozens of ponds to choose from.

Little Long Pond in May and June. The dimples on the water at dusk will make any fly fisherman smile.

Try trolling or casting spinners along the east shore of Green Pond, especially around the downed trees. Another hotspot is along the small island on Little Long Pond, often a favorite location for shore fishermen who angle for rainbows throughout the evening. The fishing remains good on these ponds due to substantial stocking by DEC. The east end of the St. Regis Canoe Area does, however, see a lot of traffic. It is very popular with day tripping canoeists, and holiday weekends can be very crowded. Overfishing in the early season can reduce fish populations, so catch and release fishing is stressed. Keep only enough for the evening meal, and you're sure to be rewarded in the future.

The west end of the St. Regis Canoe Area is centered on two large bodies of water. Long Pond, which has been mentioned, offers access to Ledge Pond, Mountain Pond, Slang Pond, Turtle Pond, Ebony Pond, Track Pond and Hoel Pond. Hoel Pond, Ledge Pond and Long Pond are known for big lake trout. The others hold decent populations of brook trout. Between Long Pond and St. Regis Pond lies the other big pond in the area, Fish Pond, with its two lean-tos on opposite shores. The tranquility this woodland pond offers is the reward most brook trout fishermen seek; the fishing is a bonus. Fish Pond is surrounded by Nellie Pond, Bessie Pond, Kit Fox Pond, Mud Pond, Little Long Pond, Little Fish Pond, Lydia Pond and Clamshell Pond and offers more solitude than any of the other large ponds in the area. It is arduous getting to Fish Pond and that tends to keep the day trippers at bay. The ponds surrounding Fish Pond all hold good populations of brook trout, with Nellie, Bessie and Clamshell Ponds clear favorites. Fishing pressure at this end of the area is heavy at times, particularly in the spring and fall. Fish Pond also produces some nice lake trout, along with a generous number of brook trout. The shoals along the west end of Fish Pond offer particularly good opportunities for lake trout in the spring. This is certainly a place to practice catch and release. Take a couple

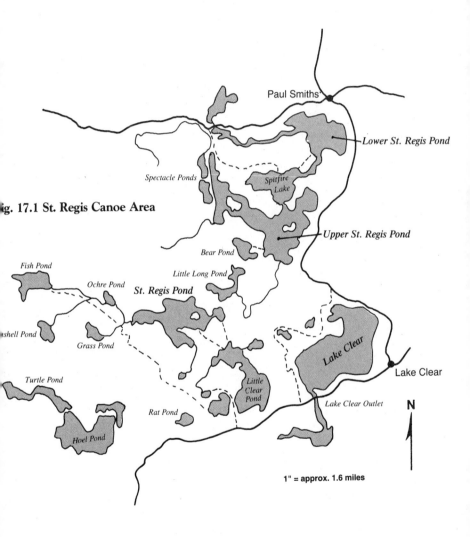

Paul Smiths

Lower St. Regis Pond

Spectacle Ponds

Spitfire Lake

ig. 17.1 St. Regis Canoe Area

Upper St. Regis Pond

Bear Pond

Little Long Pond

Fish Pond

Ochre Pond

St. Regis Pond

shell Pond

Grass Pond

Turtle Pond

Little Clear Pond

Lake Clear

Lake Clear

Rat Pond

Lake Clear Outlet

N

Hoel Pond

1" = approx. 1.6 miles

of nice fish for dinner and toss the rest back for future fishing fun. Bullheads, a fine eating fish, are plentiful in nearly all the ponds in the St. Regis Area, and can be caught all night long with a hook, sinker and worm that is cast out and left on bottom.

Advice for travelling and fishing in the St. Regis Canoe Area can be summed up in one phrase — go light.

Canoes should be very lightweight, and those rigged with oar locks for rowing are a plus. When trolling, it is essential to keep a slow speed, to present the bait to the fish; yet one must row fast enough to keep the bait from dragging bottom. Rowing allows for greater control, especially in windy conditions.

Trolling methods have proven productive for trout and are easily mastered. Try using a Lake Clear Wabbler with a snelled hook or leader trailing behind. Attached to the leader use either a nightcrawler or a streamer fly. Mickey Finn, Hornberg, Grey Ghost and Muddler Minnow are popular patterns for streamers. Trolling a streamer without the Wabbler requires that the fisherman twitch or sweep the rod to cause the streamer to dart like a wounded minnow. Real minnows are not allowed as bait in any of the St. Regis Canoe Area ponds, as some of the ponds have been reclaimed to clean out all the junk fish.

Rods should be medium action with six to eight pound test lines for trolling. Ultralight spinning rods with four pound test lines are good for casting. Fly rods should be 7½ to 8½ feet in length and should take a six to seven weight line; a sinking tip line is useful for trolling. Fly hatches are numerous and are similar to most Adirondack river hatches. The peak of the mayfly hatches is late May through early June, yet sporadic hatches occur throughout the season. Using dry flies like a Black Gnat or Adams in size 14 or 16 at dusk is often productive. Lakers have been known to feed heavily on the surface late in the day, and casting a size six to eight White Wulff or Rat Faced MacDougal will sometimes result in furious action. A favorite technique is to drift the shorelines of these ponds and cast small ⅛ to ¼ oz. spinning lures along the shore. Look for schools of fleeing minnows along the shore early and late in the day and cast the lure in front of them. A slow retrieve with a twitch of the rod every few revolutions has taken many nice fish. Many lures will work, but good results are often had with Phoebes, Mepps, C.P. Swings and Kastmasters, in gold or brass tone.

Adjacent to the St. Regis Canoe Area, but on the south side of the railroad tracks, is the Fish Creek-Rollins Pond State Campsite. The Fish Creek area offers some outstanding fishing opportunities for both cool water and cold water species. The State Camp-grounds on Fish Creek and Rollins Pond are well kept and operated by DEC. They offer a fine base camp area for day trips to the many ponds surrounding this area. Boats with motors are allowed in many of these ponds and access is often right off Rt. 30. The fishing opportunities for smallmouth and largemouth bass are excellent, and there are enough northern pike available to make things inter-esting. Some of the better cool water ponds are Follensby, Clear Pond (off Rt. 30), Copperas Pond, Square Pond, Rollins Pond and Fish Creek Ponds. One pond that has consistently produced nice catches of bass and northern pike is Floodwood Pond. Easily accessed via the Floodwood Road off Rt. 30 at Saranac Inn, the pond can offer some furious smallmouth fishing with surface pop-pers. It is one of the prime "heat of the summer" bass ponds in this area. The action trollers experience with northerns can also be sur-prising, especially at the western end of the pond near the channel to Rollins Pond. Fish surface poppers or other lures along the shoreline wherever you find downed trees and stumps. These ponds all feed into the Upper Saranac Lake, and many primitive campsites are located on the shores.

Boat and canoe rentals are also located nearby at Hickoks Boat Livery on Fish Creek Pond. Numerous roadside ponds are located in this area, and some hold decent populations of brook trout and rainbows. Whey Pond in the Fish Creek Campsite is a special trout regulations water (minimum length 12 inches, three fish per day, artificials only). It is known for its trophy rainbows and brook trout. Black Pond, located nearby, is also a good bet.

Horseshoe, Sunrise, Echo, Green, Rat and Sunday Ponds round out the list of brook trout ponds. Green Pond off Rt. 30, and also Green Pond near the State Hatchery, both hold good populations of kokanee salmon. Known as dwarf or red salmon, these little fighters rarely reach sizes over 12 inches, yet can be caught readily by trolling a wabbler and worm and are one of the best eating fish anywhere. The silvery exterior yields a bright pink interior meat that rivals any salmon for sweetness and taste.

Bass fishing has been overlooked in the Adirondacks mainly because trout and salmon are so readily available. The cool water fisheries of the Fish Creek-Saranac Area are ideal bass habitat, as are Upper and Lower St. Regis Lakes and Meacham Lake. The shorelines of these waters offer rocky shoals and numerous downed trees. This spells structure, and bass love it. Other than a large salmon, there is nothing I'd rather have on the end of a fly rod than a scrappy smallmouth bass. At the end of a hot summer day, smallmouth action can be outstanding. Using a small cork popper on a flyrod or a surface lure on a spinning rod, fish close to the shorelines of the ponds. The closer you can cast to the shore, right in among the weeds and limbs, the better your chances. As the water calms towards dusk, the big fish are often taken in the shallow areas near drop-offs to deep water. Bass in the two to three pound range are available, and the occasional northern pike will often boil out of the water for a surface plug. Best choices are cork poppers with rubber legs in green, black or yellow, or surface Rapalas, Rebels and frog imitations. Fishing crankbaits or leadhead jigs with rubber worms in the deeper water will produce fish in the heat of the day. Minnows either trolled or cast with a bobber to shore will do well, especially for pike. Unfortunately, most all pike will take live bait deep, making releasing fish difficult. Although minnows produce well, so many small pike are killed in the releasing of them that minnows should be reserved as a last resort when all else fails.

An area that rivals the St. Regis Canoe Area for beauty and solitude is the Bog River Flow Wilderness Area. Located in St. Lawrence

County, just west of Tupper Lake, this area is accessed via Rt. 471 off Rt. 30 south of Tupper Lake. The turnoff to Horseshoe Lake-Veterans Mountain Camp leads around Horseshoe Lake six miles to a dirt road that dead ends at the state launch on the lower dam of the Bog River. This large tract includes the Bog River Flow which connects Hitchins Pond, Lows Lake, Grassy Pond, Tomar Pond and several other natural ponds which were back-flooded as a result of the creation of the upper dam on Lows Lake. A very large, but quite shallow body of water, with an average depth of eight to ten feet, Lows Lake is very susceptible to heavy waves. Even with a light wind the lake can whitecap, and with the prevalent western winds not blocked by any large mountains, Lows Lake can often be unnavigable by canoe.

The launch at the lower dam leads one upriver two miles to Hitchins Pond. Another shallow body of water, Hitchins rarely gets as rough as Lows Lake. It contains brook trout and yellow perch; however, the trout are only fishable in the very early season. As soon as the water warms enough for the perch to become active, an angler cannot get through the perch to get at the brookies. The perch, some as large as 1½ lbs. and 16 inches long, can provide plenty of action for the kids, and if prepared as "poor man's shrimp," they make a wonderful meal for adults. They are easily caught on spinners, or hook and worm. A short carry at the head of Hitchins Pond leads over the upper dam and into Lows Lake. The first seven miles up the flow are quite narrow and not often windy. Once you get past the Boy Scout Camp on the right shore, the lake begins to widen until a second narrow passage is reached about one mile further along. Once through this channel, a view of Lows Lake proper is achieved, and you are greeted with the usual white-capped waves. Lows Lake is speckled with several beautiful islands, but camping is limited to a few numbered sites. The majority of the island campsites are reserved for Boy Scout use in June, July and August. Grassy Pond, located near the head of Lows Lake, offers true remoteness and a feeling of real wilderness. Grassy Pond Mountain, with its soaring cliffs,

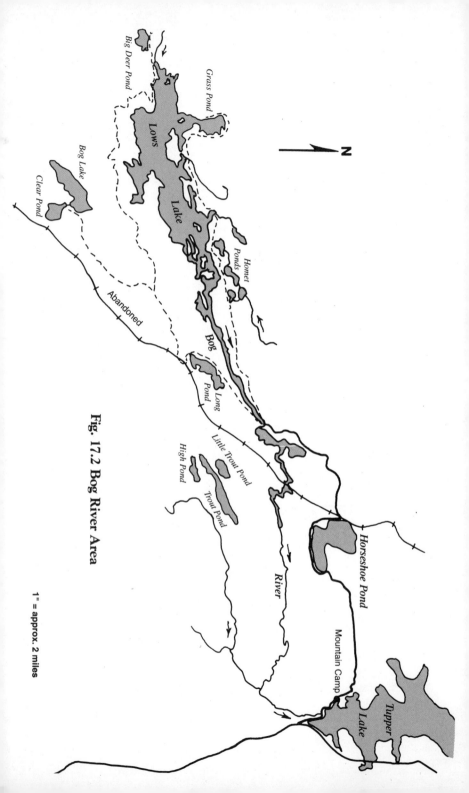

Fig. 17.2 Bog River Area

1" = approx. 2 miles

is a known nesting site for bald and golden eagles. Eagles are often spotted on Lows Lake, along with large numbers of loons which breed in this area. Coyotes and owls usually are heard during the evening, and moose have been spotted in the area.

The fishing on Lows Lake, Grassy Pond and the Bog River is quite good for brook trout. Because the wind is so often a problem, trolling can be difficult yet it is effective. Spinners cast along shorelines can produce nice catches, as can well presented dry flies during a hatch. Best bets are to cover shorelines in stumpy areas, or along the cobblestoned islands. The trout seem to slack off by late June as the water warms, but pick up again in the month of September. I find that trout fishing on the lakes and ponds falls into several distinct time frames, in regards to peak production. Ideally, the best time to fish brook trout is right after the ice goes off the pond. Generally, this is late April or early May in the northern Adirondacks but the amount of snowfall and extremes of winter temperatures affect ice-out dates drastically. In a five year span, ice-out on the ponds has ranged from March 28 to May 7. Predicting the day the ice will go is difficult at best; even so, the first weekend in May is often a safe bet for good fishing.

Brook trout feed heavily and respond favorably to just about anything tossed their way for the first week to ten days after ice-out. Unfortunately, this feeding frenzy leads into what I call the "two week doldrums." Some ponds may produce for two days after ice-out, some up to ten days. Yet after this initial strong feeding period, the trout can then go off their feed for up to two weeks. The end of the doldrums is marked by the first few hatches of the season and is over for sure once the dragonfly nymphs are out. Consistently, the weekend of Mothers Day in early May has produced the finest fishing of the year. Hatches continue throughout May and June, and the trout remain on the feed. As the heat of the summer comes upon the ponds, the water warms and trout seek deeper, cooler water. Often they congregate on the spring holes or in the area of feeder streams on the ponds. Usually, the depth of the water the fish are in negates trolling, so still fishing is the order of the day. July and August bring the hottest weather, and trout fishing is reduced to early morning or early evening trips in search of rising trout. This period need not be a fishless one, however, as bass and pike can be taken readily in deep water during the day, and along the shoreline at dusk. The trout fishing picks up in September, and is very good as the cool fall nights lower the water temperature. A fat fall brook trout in spawning colors offers a splendid complement to the spectacular autumn foliage. The warm days and cool nights make for enjoyable camping, and there are no bugs and fewer people in the woods after Labor Day.

Joe Hackett has owned and operated Tahawus Guide Service and Backcountry Outfitters, Ltd., since 1978. He grew up in Elizabethtown, New York, fishing the Boquet River. After earning a Masters in Recreation/Outdoor Education in 1980, Joe was a co-founder of the New York State Outdoor Guides Association and today specializes in fly fishing remote ponds for brook trout. The St. Regis Canoe Area is one of the regions he knows best.

18

THE
ST. LAWRENCE
RIVER

by Allen Benas

Serving as a common border between the United States and Canada for a touch over 100 miles, the St Lawrence River has invitingly beckoned to freshwater fishermen in both nations for centuries. This majestic river, one of the longest in the continental United States, provides year round fishing enjoyment for the whole family.

The St. Lawrence Seaway has been referred to as one of the most dramatic engineering undertakings of the century. With its completion in 1959, this conduit to the sea helped create the longest inland waterway on our planet. Ships from around the world now penetrate half a continent, while power generated by the great river supplies vast areas of both New York State and the Canadian Province of Ontario.

To musky hunters the world over, the river is considered Mecca. The present world record muskellunge was taken here in 1957, by the legendary Arthur Lawton. To professional angling organizations such as the Bass Anglers Sportsmen's Society, the river holds more bass per acre than any other place they hold contests.

To those simply intent on having an enjoyable vacation, the river offers unrivaled scenic beauty, unlimited cruising opportunities, the near certainty of catching fish, and a relaxed life style that is unparalleled by more confined and crowded vacation areas.

The river, named after the Saint honored on the day of its discovery in 1615, is 568 miles long from its source at the eastern end of Lake Ontario to the Gulf of St. Lawrence. The river's primary recreational area is contained within the first 90 miles, from Lake Ontario to Massena, N.Y. From the beautiful village of Massena downstream, the river is little more than a ditch as it leads to Montreal, Quebec City, and on to the Gulf.

At its source at Lake Ontario, the river is over 20 miles across. Dotted here by over 1,700 islands of every size and description, it gradually narrows to only a few miles wide in its first 35 miles of flow. This expanse of water misled the earliest french explorer, Jacques Cartier, to name the region Lac Des Mille Isles, or Lake of the Thousand islands. It is this section, now an extremely popular vacation and resort region known as the Thousand Islands, that has established the river as an angler's paradise.

Although populated by a wide array of fresh water fish, the river's reputation as a premier sport fishery centers around four major species: great northern pike, smallmouth bass, walleye and muskellunge. Seasons for these vary, so anglers can be on the river from early May through mid March.

As the river begins to run fresh in the spring, usually in early April, fishermen anxiously await the opening of the northern pike season on the first Saturday in May. The success on opening day will depend heavily on what kind of spring the area had. A cold spring can set back the spawn, meaning the mature pike could still be in the shallows of the marshes, safe from the angler's lure. A warming, or "normal" spring beginning in early April, means "business as usual."

Although an immense water area, the St. Lawrence attracts boats of every size. Given calm winds and a sense of stable weather, anglers in boats as small as 14 feet are a common sight.

Should the wind increase, the numerous islands offer shelter and the waters surrounding them can be productive.

Knowledgeable pike anglers will seek out locations where they know of underwater weed growth. This knowledge is based on fishing experience during previous summer months when the weeds grow to the surface, or on time spent studying charts of the river that show areas of changing depth, which are common sites of weed growth. The weeds provide green cover speckled by flickering sunlight and shadows created by wave action that camouflage this efficient predator. The northern lies in hiding, awaiting the unsuspecting passer-by. Like other members of the Esox genus, the pike is an ambush hunter.

The most successful pike anglers use large, silver shiners, available locally although imported from Arkansas. They are usually drifted along the outside edge of the weedbeds, just off the river bottom about 20 feet down. Seldom will a pike pass up an opportunity for this tender morsel. Often, deep running artificial lures are productive. Dardevle spoons, deep running crankbaits and jigs with worm and twister tails, either pork or plastic, have established reputable stature in the northern pike arsenal.

Well traveled anglers often compare northern pike fishing in the St. Lawrence with other areas. The consensus is that larger fish, although in smaller numbers, can still be caught farther north, in Canada. But when it comes to quantity, the St. Lawrence shines. Limit catches of fish averaging four to five pounds (with occasional trophies in the 10 to 15 pound class) are often the rule.

Northern pike are a popular attraction for ice fishermen from freeze-up usually in early January, until the season closes in March. Specimens as large as 20 pounds are not unheard of during the winter months, when the largest pike of the year are usually caught. Popular wintertime northern pike hangouts can be found at Wilson Hill Causeway between Louisville and Massena off Route 37B; Coles Creek Marina between Waddington and Massena on Route 37; Brandy Brook, just east of Waddington on Route 37; the pulp docks in Ogdensburg (east of the old Diamond National Plant); Perch Bay outside Morristown off Route 37; and Chippewa Bay. Early season, open water pike fishing can also be quite good in the waters mentioned, as they will produce numerous post-spawn fish. Often overlooked, boat marinas offer outstanding early season pike fishing. You can find marina facilities in nearly every community along the St. Lawrence.

The season for northern pike extends from early May through March 15th of the following year. It then closes for seven weeks to allow for the spawn. The pike season is the longest of all sport fishing seasons on the river.

It is hard to say which fish is most synonymous with the St. Lawrence: the musky or the smallmouth bass. But there is no doubt that the smallmouth is far more abundant, being found in large numbers from Cape Vincent to Massena.

No native needs a calendar to tell when the third Saturday in June has arrived. This is the heaviest traffic day of the year with cars, vans, campers and boat trailers all heading for the river. Ask any old-timer along the river when the tourist season starts and he'll more than likely say "when bass season opens!"

Many things make bass the most sought after of all the river species. First, they are spectacular fighters. Pound for pound they are the fightingest fish that swims, as the expression goes. Second, successful bass fishing takes real thought and skill.

Throughout the summer months bass will move constantly, from day to day, even hour to hour. Weather fronts will affect them more than any other species, as will sunlight and cloud cover. One day they will be deep, the next, shallow. You might catch them in 20 feet in the morning, but have to go down 120 feet in the afternoon. Any self-professed bass expert you hear of along the St. Lawrence is probably giving himself a lot more credit than he should. Bass, simply put, are intimidating fish; they can make fools out of the best anglers. That's probably the main reason why sports love to go after them.

The St. Lawrence Valley was created by glaciation eons ago,

during the ice ages. Consequently, there is no such thing as an average depth. With the deepest spot being nearly 300 feet, with adjacent islands only a few yards away, you can appreciate how a 30-foot boat can have its bow in one foot of water while anglers fish in 25 feet off the stern. Where modern crankbaits, for example, may serve well in impoundments, we have found it nearly impossible to get them down to the 50-foot-plus depths that hold bass during the hot summer months.

Early in the season, while bass are still in the shallows, artificials can be very effective. After they move into deeper water, artificials are most practical in the evenings, when the bass move into the shallows to feed. Successful casting of artificials is done in depths ranging from a few to no more than 15 feet of water. Evening casting is best in bays or along the shoreline and around docks. The most popular artificials among visiting pros are jig 'n pig, medium size spinnerbaits and small crankbaits.

As with the pike fishing, the most successful anglers will use shiners. These two to three-inch-long baitfish will produce more fish than all lures combined. Think of it this way: How can you improve on the fish's natural food?

For both pike and bass, tackle used ranges from ultralight to medium weight. A good bet for a sporting encounter with either species would be a light action rod and reel with a capacity for at least 175 yards of six pound monofilament line. With pike, a stronger leader is suggested not so much for pulling strength as for protection from their ultra sharp teeth.

Favorite smallie waters along the St. Lawrence can be found starting near Cape Vincent midway up the north side of Grenadier Island (especially after a north wind); the shoal on the N.W. corner between Haddock and Grenadier Island (good late summer fishing); Wilson Bay (south of Tibbetts Point Lighthouse); and the waters between Fox Island and the mainland. Moving east (downriver), numerous shoals and weed beds along Clayton and Alexandria Bay hold large populations of bass. Farther down-

Giant muskies like this still swim in the St. Lawrence, where Arthur Lawton once took fresh water angling's most revered record: a monster muskellunge one ounce short of 70 pounds.

river, smallmouth bass can be found along any current break or weed bed between Morristown, Ogdensburg, Waddington, Louisville and Massena.

Pike and bass remain the most popular of the St. Lawrence fishes throughout the summer months. As mid September approaches with its typically shorter days and cooling nights, however, there is another group of anglers who begin to appear on the scene. Decked out in heavy garb, braving the chilled river in boats ranging in size from 16 to 25 feet, these anglers are in search of the ultimate fresh water trophy. These are the "Musky Men."

To some, the musky is the "fish of 10,000 casts," to others, the fish of 1,000 hours. To no one is it an easy gamefish. There is no question that the muskellunge fishery here has certain problems, and that very large specimens are less common than they once were. Yet the St. Lawrence still offers one of the best opportunities to boat a couple of these revered, almost mystical battlers.

What makes the St. Lawrence still a choice musky fishing destination? One reason may be that it holds the largest of the two remaining natural, or unstocked, strains of muskellunge left in North America. Another may be the knowledge that the present world record muskellunge came from this water.

Many suggest that having withstood the test of time for over thirty five years, the late Arthur Lawton's 69 pound 15 ounce record may well stand forever. Anglers, however, are not as intent on breaking Lawton's record as they are on setting their own. Perhaps they are after their first legal size fish, a personal record in itself. Maybe a thirty plus pounder is what they're after — small, perhaps, in comparison to Lawton's, but a very respectable trophy nevertheless. Maybe even a seasoned Musky Man comes to see the expression on his son's or grandson's face as he catches his first musky, making him a member of perhaps the most exclusive fraternity of fresh water anglers. All these are records when you are a musky hunter.

The range of the St. Lawrence musky, both as a species and individually, is the largest of all this river's gamefish. They are found everywhere between Lake Ontario and Massena. The three most popular areas, however, remain the Thousand Islands region, where Lawton's record fish fell, around the city of Ogdensburg, and below the village of Massena.

In 1984 a study to learn more about the unique St. Lawrence river strain of muskellunge was intitiated by SUNY College of Forestry at Syracuse. Netting in suspected spawning locations yielded several specimens. While most were scale sampled, tagged and released, nearly three dozen were fitted with external transmitters. These radiotelemetry devices allowed biologists to trace the movements of muskies in this vast waterway.

What the biologists found was previously unsuspected by all but a few experienced musky fishing guides. The St. Lawrence River muskies are travelers; they are migratory. Mature fish tend to spawn in the same bay every year, but after the spawn they leave the area for larger ranges. Most Thousand Islands muskies summer in the upper St. Lawrence and eastern Lake Ontario.

Part of the muskellunge strategy is timing. Most musky fishing is done in the fall. The fish are at the height of their aggressiveness, gorging themselves in anticipation of the lean winter months that lie ahead. Musky mania prevails along the St. Lawrence from mid September until the season closes on November 31st.

By far, the majority of muskies are taken by trolling. Large lures are trolled at speeds that make them perform at the peak of their intended design. Many veteran musky anglers will tell you "it doesn't make much difference if the lure moves like a fish, as long as it moves like it's crazy." Every seasoned musky fisherman I know contends that the color of a lure is secondary. It is the action that drives them nuts, and nutty fish make mistakes.

The most successful lures have two or three sections and are from six to nine inches long. For years the majority of muskies were taken on the then popular Creek Chub lures, which worked well with the heavy monel line that was used to get the lures down to depths of 20 feet. With the gaining popularity of downriggers, which permit much lighter tackle and thus more sport, these have now been replaced in popularity by a multi-sectioned lure manufactured by the Radtke Bait Company. Although this lure takes a great many Thousand Island muskies, others such as the Believer, Cisco Kid, Rapala and Water Dog work well on downriggers, and chalk up success year in and year out.

Among the most popular musky fishing spots along the St. Lawrence are the waters off Cape Vincent, including Featherbed and Hinkley Shoals. Downriver towards Clayton, anglers congregate on the famous 40 Acre Shoals, Gananoque Narrows and just west of the international bridge in the fast flowing water adjacent to the shipping channel. Still further downstream, the area around Chippewa Bay, although treacherous to even experienced boaters, is a known musky hangout. Below Chippewa Bay you enter the Brockville Narrows where musky fishermen also converge.

At Ogdensburg, most musky fishing activity centers around the sandbar where the Oswegatchie River empties into the St. Lawrence, just upstream from the international bridge. This is the only place along the entire river where most fishing is done at night. This rare occurrence stems not only from the movements of fish (which come in to feed when the sun goes down) but also from the fact that the more prominent guides have daytime jobs, and can only fish at night. Regardless, night fishing here produces.

The farthest east that musky fishing is done is in Lake St. Lawrence, both above and below the St. Lawrence/FDR Power Dam located just outside Massena. Above the dam musky fishermen concentrate their activities near Coles Creek, Wilson Hill and Long Sault Islands. Below the dam most musky hunters key in on the tailrace on the American side. Here, numerous muskies are caught and released on a regular basis. Trolling one or two lures per angler, depending on whether you are fishing in Ontario or New York waters, fishermen follow underwater contours in depths ranging from 18 to as deep as 60 feet. Days can be spent with not even a hit. On the other hand, occasionally a boat will limit out in only a few hours. In comparison to musky fishing, a crap shoot is a sure thing.

In addition to the three species just discussed, the upper St. Lawrence holds a promising population of walleye. Possibly due in part to lack of angler pressure, walleyes have been allowed to multiply and grow to near record size. Seven and eight pounders are average here, and 12 to 15 pounders are trophies (when was the last time you threw back a six pound walleye?) The most successful spring walleye fishing is done in shallow bays in May and June, by those casting Rapalas, small crankbaits and jigs tipped with worms. During late July and August activity centers between the shipping channel and adjacent shallower areas, where the fish are intercepted with jigs and nightcrawlers as they head into the shallows to feed in the dark.

The most popular walleye spots are Carleton Island near Cape Vincent, NY and Fishers Landing, NY, just west of the Thousand Islands Bridge. The mouth of the Oswegatchie River in Ogdensburg has started producing good catches of walleye. Within the past few years, the waters between Waddington and Massena have also produced outstanding catches of large walleye. Of course, one of the premier walleye fishing grounds has to be below the St. Lawrence/FDR Power Project. Here, fishing is done exclusively from boats. Most walleye are concentrated in the tailrace of the dam and early morning and early evening seem to be the best times.

For non angling members of the family, dozens of attractions will provide hours and even days of activity while the fishermen enjoy their sport. The St. Lawrence River makes the area an international playground shared by Americans, Canadians and visitors from around the world. They come to cruise, and they come to camp. Many come for the numerous attractions. But by far, most come to fish the waters of this bountiful boundary.

N.Y.S. DEPARTMENT OF ENVIRONMENTAL CONSERVATION OFFICES IN THE ADIRONDACKS

Information on camping, boating, hunting, fishing, trapping, fish and wildlife, forestry, plants, etc. Numerous free pamphlets available. New York State Headquarters: 50 Wolf Road, Albany, NY 12233. Offices for Regions 5 and 6 (see map), which serve the various Adirondack counties, are listed below.

REGION 5

Headquarters:
Ray Brook, NY 12977
(518) 891-1370.

Sub-Headquarters:
Hudson Street
Box 220
Warrensburg, NY 12885
(518) 623-3671

Forestry Offices:
Clinton, Essex, Franklin
Counties
Ray Brook, NY 12977
(518) 891-1370

Saratoga, Warren,
Washington Counties
Hudson Street
Box 220
Warrensburg, NY 12885
(518) 623-3671

Fulton, Hamilton Counties
Northville, NY 12134
(518) 863-4545

REGION 6

Headquarters:
State Office Building
317 Washington Street
Watertown, NY 13601
(315) 782-0100

Sub-headquarters:
State Office Building
Utica, NY 13501
(315) 797-6120

Forestry Offices:

Jefferson , Lewis Counties
Rt. 812
P.O. Box 31
Lowville, NY 13367
(315) 376-3521

St. Lawrence County
30 Court St.
Canton, NY 13617
(315) 386-4546

Herkimer, Oneida Counties
225 North Main Street
Herkimer, NY 13350
(315) 866-6330

34 LARGEST ADIRONDACK LAKES

COUNTY	NAME OF WATER	NO. OF ACRES
Essex-Clinton	Lake Champlain*	281,600
Warren	Lake George	28,100
Fulton-Saratoga	Great Sacandaga Lake*	26,656
St. Lawrence	Cranberry Lake	6,976
St. Lawrence	Carry Falls Reservoir	6,458
Franklin	Tupper Lake	6,240
Herkimer	Stillwater Reservoir	6,195
Hamilton	Raquette Lake	5,274
Franklin	Upper Saranac lake	5,056
Hamilton	Indian Lake	4,365
Essex	Schroon Lake	4,128
Hamilton	Long Lake	4,090
Hamilton	Piseco Lake	2,848
Essex	Lake Placid	2,803
Herkimer	Hinckley Reservoir*	2,784
Clinton	Upper Chateaugay Lake	2,605
Hamilton	Little Tupper Lake	2,381
Franklin	Lower Saranac Lake	2,285
Herkimer	Fourth Lake (Fulton Chain)	2,138
Clinton	Chazy Lake	1,606
Hamilton	Sacandaga Lake	1,600
Hamilton	Lake Pleasant	1,440
Hamilton	Lake Lila	1,424
Franklin	Middle Saranac Lake	1,376
Franklin	Union Falls Flow	1,376
Warren	Brant Lake	1,376
Fulton	Peck Lake	1,370
Herkimer	Big Moose Lake	1,286
Hamilton	Blue Mountain Lake	1,261
Hamilton	Forked Lake	1,248
Franklin	Meacham Lake	1,203
Herkimer	Woodhull Lake	1,158
Hamilton	Abanakee Lake	1,018
Franklin	Lake Clear	1,000

* Parts of these lakes lie outside the Adirondack Park.
  Source: Adirondack Park Agency.

ADIRONDACK RIVER CLASSIFICATIONS

RIVER	WILD	SCENIC	RECREATIONAL
Ampersand Brook		8.0 mi.	
Ausable—Main Branch			22.0
Ausable—East Branch		9.0	28.3
Ausable—West Branch			34.5
Black		7.8	
Bog		7.3	
Boreas		11.5	
Bouquet			47.7
Bouquet—North Fork		6.0	
Bouquet—South Fork		5.5	
Blue Mt. Stream		9.0	
Cedar	14.3	15.0	11.0
Cold	14.0		
Deer		6.2	
East Canada Creek		20.9	
Grasse—Middle Branch		14.5	
Grasse—North Branch		25.4	
Grasse—South Branch		38.9	5.2
Hudson	10.5	13.0	58.6
Independence		26.0	0.5
Indian (Tributary of Hudson R.)			8.3
Indian (Trib. of Moose R., S. Branch)	13.0		
Jordan		18.0	
Kunjamuk	8.0	10.4	
Long Pond Outlet		16.0	
Marion		5.0	
Moose—Main Branch		15.8	
Moose—South Branch		38.9	
Opalescent	11.0		
Oswegatchie—Main Branch	18.5		
Oswegatchie—Middle Branch	14.5	23.4	
Oswegatchie—West Branch		7.0	6.1
Otter Brook		10.0	
Ouluska Pass Brook	3.0		
Piseco Outlet	4.2		
Raquette		33.8	39.0
Red		9.7	
Rock		6.9	1.2
Round Lake Outlet	2.7		
St. Regis—East Branch		14.5	6.1
St. Regis—Main Branch		15.5	25.0
St. Regis—West Branch		35.0	5.5
Sacandaga—East Branch	11.5		14.0
Sacandaga—Main Branch			31.0
Sacandaga—West Branch	18.7		17.8
Salmon			12.3
Saranac			60.4
Schroon			66.7
West Canada Creek	8.0	17.0	11.0
West Canada Creek—S. Branch	5.9		9.7
West Stony Creek		7.7	8.7
TOTALS	155.1	511.3	539.5
TOTAL MILES CLASSIFIED	1205.9		

Index

INDEX

About the Good Fishing
In New York Series

What state in the union has 4,000 lakes over 6.4 acres in size? Or 3,400,000 total acres of lakes? Or 70,000 miles of rivers, 15,000 of these supporting trout?

And what state has 1,200,000 acres of coastal water? Or 1,850 miles of coastline?

The answer is, only New York State has all of this in combination.

We believe, in fact, that New York State offers the best fishing of any state in the country, and it is oh so wonderfully close to so many people.

But let's get a little more specific. Where else can you find together all this: Hundreds of miles of shoreline on two Great Lakes; over a hundred more miles of shoreline on the sixth largest lake in the country (Lake Champlain); a magnificent and biologically rich great estuary (the Hudson); not one but two major mountain ranges (the Catskills and the Adirondacks); a virtual cornucopia of coastal waters, including bays, inlets, cuts, islands, points, and immense Long Island Sound; a beautiful heartland laced with huge, clean, deep, glacially-formed lakes (the one and only Finger Lakes Region); America's "Most Beautiful Lake" (Lake George); intriguing tidal rivers where sea-run trout abound; tens of thousands of acres of clean and undeveloped watershed reservoirs; plus many other surprises?

The answer is, of course, only in New York State.

With the amazing amount of fishing available in the Empire State, a series of five comprehensive guidebooks was not only justified but, we felt, long overdue. We believe each book in this series to be of the highest quality, both in terms of editorial content and graphic support. Each contributing author is a true expert on his particular subject. In most cases, the authors live in the area they have written about and have ten, twenty or more years of actual fishing experience on the waters they discuss. There are no armchair experts connected with this series of books at all.

The accurate text is supported by dozens of professional, usable maps, plus dozens more photos, charts and other illustrations.

These are true guidebooks, and the 8¼" by 5½" size lets them go easily along in glove compartment or tackle bag.

I hope you will look for each of the five volumes in the Good Fishing in New York Series (the map on the back cover of each book shows the geographical break-down of the series). And I hope you will actually use these books, and take them with you, to help you explore the best fishing that America has to offer — right here in beautiful New York State.

— Jim Capossela,
creator of the *Good Fishing In New York Series*

❦

Good Fishing Close to New York City (Revised edition planned for 1993) — Covers all of southern New York, Long Island, Western Long Island Sound, and the New York Bight — fresh water and salt water! Complete, detailed coverage of the Croton Watershed. By Jim Capossela

Great Fishing in Lake Ontario & Tributaries (Revised edition planned for 1993) — From 40 pound king salmon to giant brown and rainbow trout, from steelhead in the tributaries to ice fishing for perch — everything you need to know about this extraordinary resource. By Rich Giessuebel.

Good Fishing in the Catskills — The one and only comprehensive guide to the legendary trout rivers of the Catskills. Special sections on lakes and reservoirs. Bonus: Otsego County, the Mohawk River and the Capital District. By Jim Capossela, with other contributors.

Good Fishing in the Adirondacks — An in-depth angling guide to the great wilderness of the East. Sixteen local authors take you along to waters large and small, from Lake Champlain to the St. Lawrence River and Tug Hill. Dennis Aprill, Editor.

Good Fishing in Western New York — A revealing guide to the little known waters of the western tier. Ten chapters explore all that the majestic Finger Lakes have to offer. Other chapters discuss dozens more streams and rivers, lakes, and ponds. C. Scott Sampson, Editor.

Also from The Countryman Press and Backcountry Publications

The Countryman Press and its associated companies, long known for fine books on the outdoors, offer a range of practical and readable manuals for sportsmen and women.

Fishing

Fishing Small Streams with a Fly Rod, by Charles R. Meck, $14.95 (paper), $24.95 (deluxe cloth edition)

Fishing Vermont's Streams and Lakes, by Peter Cammann, $13.00

Good Fishing in the Catskills: From the Waters of the Capital District to the Delaware River, by Jim Capossela, $15.00

Good Fishing in Western New York: The Finger Lakes and Other Waters, from Oneida Lake to Chautauqua Lake, edited by C. Scott Sampson, $15.00

Ice Fishing, by Jim Capossela, $15.00

Pennsylvania Trout Streams and Their Hatches, by Charles R. Meck, $14.95

Virginia Trout Streams, by Harry Slone, $14.95

Fly Tying

Bass Flies, by Dick Stewart, $12.95 (paper), $19.95 (cloth)

Fly Tying Tips, edited by Dick Stewart, $9.95

The Orvis Guide to Beginning Fly Tying, by Eric Leiser, $9.95

Universal Fly Tying Guide, by Dick Stewart, $9.95

Discover the Adirondacks Series

A series of four-season, multi-use guides to off-the-beaten-path outdoor recreation.

Discover the Adirondack High Peaks, $14.95

Discover the Central Adirondacks, $12.95

Discover the Eastern Adirondacks, $10.95

Discover the Northeastern Adirondacks, $9.95

Discover the Northern Adirondacks, $12.95

Discover the Northwestern Adirondacks, $12.95

Discover the South Central Adirondacks, $10.95

Discover the Southeastern Adirondacks, $9.95

Discover the Southern Adirondacks, $10.95

Discover the Southwestern Adirondacks, $9.95

Discover the West Central Adirondacks, $14.95

Other books for Adirondack residents and visitors:

Fifty Hikes in the Adirondacks, by Barbara McMartin, $12.95

Adirondack Cross-Country Skiing, by Dennis Conroy with Shirley Matzke, $16.00

We also publish guides to canoeing, hiking, walking, bicycling, and ski touring in New England, the Mid-Atlantic states, and the Midwest.

Our titles are available in bookshops and in many sporting goods stores, or they may be ordered directly from the publisher. When ordering by mail, please add $2.50 per order for shipping and handling. To order or obtain a complete catalog, please write The Countryman Press, Inc., Dept. APB, P.O. Box 175, Woodstock, Vermont 05091.